FREE GRACE THEOLOGY

5 WAYS IT
MAGNIFIES
THE GOSPEL

CHARLIE BING
JODY DILLOW
JEREMY EDMONDSON
ROGER FANKHAUSER
GRANT HAWLEY

BoldGRACE

Copyright © 2016 Bold Grace Ministries

410 N Bonham Dr.
Allen, TX 75013
www.boldgrace.org

Library of Congress Cataloging in Publication Data

Hawley, Grant Cameron (1981-), Editor
Free Grace Theology: 5 Ways It Magnifies the Gospel

1. Salvation. 2. Soteriology. 3. Free Grace.
4. Assurance. 5. Theology. I. Title.

ISBN: 978-0-9899665-4-2

Cover Design: Bold Grace Ministries
Typesetting: Holly Melton

Unless otherwise noted, all Scripture taken from the English
Standard Version of the Bible. Copyright © 2001 by Crossway
Books/Good News Publishers. All rights reserved.

Printed in the United States of America

This book is dedicated with adoring affection to the Son of God, the Lord Jesus Christ, our Savior, who died for our sins and rose from the grave. *Soli Deo Gloria.*

TABLE OF CONTENTS

Editor's Preface

Well known writer and theologian, Dr. Wayne Grudem, reopened the discussion about Free Grace theology with his recently published book, *"Free Grace" Theology: 5 Ways It Diminishes the Gospel.*[1] In it, Dr. Grudem made several accusations: (1) The Free Grace Movement does not teach the Reformation doctrine of "Justification by Faith Alone." (2) Free Grace theology weakens the gospel by avoiding any call to unbelievers to repent of their sins. (3) Free Grace theology gives false assurance of eternal life to many people who profess faith in Christ but then show no evidence in their pattern of life. (4) Free Grace teaching overemphasizes agreement with facts and underemphasizes heartfelt trust in the person of Christ. (5) Free Grace advocates have to adopt numerous highly unlikely interpretations in the New Testament because of the need to defend their mistaken understanding of the word *"alone"* in the phrase "faith alone."

This book is not intended to be a point-by-point response to Dr. Grudem's arguments. Other scholars in the Free Grace community are working on responses that will do just that. Instead, in this book, we intend to reframe the conversation. Each of the chapters of this book correspond and contrast with the chapters in Dr. Grudem's book, and each shows that, far from *diminishing* the gospel, Free Grace theology *magnifies* it. It is our hope that after reading this book, you, our dear reader, will be rejoicing with us in the freeness of the gift of everlasting life.

As with any collaboration book, there is some diversity of views expressed. The viewpoints expressed in this book are those of the respective authors.

It has been a tremendous privilege to work with Pastor Jeremy Edmondson and Drs. Charles C. Bing, Jody Dillow, and Roger Fankhauser, in the writing and publishing of this book. I am thankful for each of these godly men for their excellent contributions to this work and for their tireless labor in sharing the gospel of God's free grace and in making disciples.

---

[1] Wayne Grudem, *"Free Grace" Theology: 5 Ways It Diminishes the Gospel* (Wheaton, IL: Crossway, 2016).

FOREWORD

By David R. Anderson

Wayne Grudem's recent book, *"Free Grace" Theology: Five Ways It Diminishes the Gospel*, has slipped in under the door of the front office of evangelical theology somewhat innocuously in that it is a brief attempt to discredit the theology of Lewis Sperry Chafer, Charles Ryrie, Dwight Pentecost, Howard Hendricks, Zane Hodges, and several of their lesser-known students. The men called to task by Grudem (Bob Wilkin, Charlie Bing, Fred Lybrand, Dave Anderson, Fred Chay, and Jody Dillow) all learned their theology directly or indirectly from the professors mentioned at Dallas Theological Seminary. But Grudem is careful not to mention Chafer, Ryrie, Pentecost, or Hendricks. One has to wonder if Grudem would really say the theology of this group of luminaries would diminish the gospel.

But does the charge hold? Grudem acknowledges the gospel taught by the proponents of Free Grace theology is not a false gospel. He claims to know many, many people who have come to what he would call "saving faith" through the Free Grace gospel. He calls them "brothers," who are in dire need of some brotherly advice. Alas, though their gospel is sufficient to open the gates of heaven for those who believe it, it sadly diminishes the gospel so as to make repentance perfunctory, faith insufficient, and promotes too much reliance on the cross of Christ instead of the person of Christ. How diminished does the gospel have to be before it is a false gospel?

Grudem's book evokes a response from those whose theology he tries to undermine. Drs. Chafer, Ryrie, Pentecost, and Hendricks are not around to respond themselves. Nevertheless, those who have followed in their stead have done an admirable job to set the record straight. Rather than diminishing the gospel, these men turn the tables by arguing that Free Grace theology magnifies the gospel.

Grudem appeals repeatedly to the history of the Reformation to buttress his Reformed theology. Unfortunately, he treats the history of the

Reformed tradition much the way Catholics treat the traditions of their faith, on a plane of authority as high or even higher at times than Scripture itself. Ironically, the Reformers were trying to debunk their church traditions in favor of the Scriptures alone. Jeremy Edmondson does an admirable job of demonstrating that Reformed theology comes with Roman Catholic trappings. In so doing, the vestiges of a works-based theology for salvation has become part of the fabric of Reformed theology. In the early decades of the Reformation we witnessed the divorce and remarriage of justification and sanctification to the point that, in many respects, we are right back to Catholicism. Hence, Edmondson concludes, it is a dangerous thing to make such a strong appeal to Reformed tradition. Instead, we must keep Scripture as our sole authority.

One of the big issues as the Reformation transitioned from John Calvin to Theodore Beza during the 1560s was the source of our assurance of having eternal life. The shift went from an external focus on the Person and work of Christ (Calvin) to an internal, self-evaluation of one's faith to see if it is of the proper quality and quantity to spring the pearly gates (Beza). A major part of this shift was a greater focus on the professing believer's fruit/works and the continuance therein. Grant Hawley explains how this shift actually "diminishes grace's power to produce humility and thankfulness." After all, if I must look to my own works to see if my faith is of the proper order, am I not shifting the focus away from the Savior to myself, even if we argue that the necessary works are motivated and empowered by Christ (Alan Stanley)? By promoting our humility and thankfulness, Free Grace theology teaches us to turn from sin, and thus, magnifies the gospel.

Many have noted that the agreement between Free Grace theologians and Reformed theologians is greater than their disagreements. The sticking points seem to be the nature of faith and the source of our assurance. Charlie Bing presents an excellent chapter on assurance in which he argues that any assurance based on my level of commitment, repentance, good works, or faith is bound to be subjective and, therefore, relative. Can one have absolute assurance of one's salvation in this life? Not if Wayne Grudem is right. He has a chart in his book in which he shows how we can go from *weak* assurance to *strong* assurance as we continue to persevere in our walk with Christ. However, his system cannot provide *absolute* assurance since he believes a person must persevere to the end of his life as a faithful believer or he never was elect. Bing shows how this approach leaves the believer in the quicksand of insecurity and fear about his ultimate salvation.

An old controversy from the days of Augustine was *synergism* versus *monergism*. That just means God and man working together to effect man's salvation (*synergism*) or God working alone to bring about man's salvation (*monergism*). Reformed theologians like Grudem usually point out that God and the gospel get more glory in a *monergistic* system such as theirs than a *synergistic* system exemplified by the Arminians, since in their system man seems to be helping God along with his good works on the path to heaven. Roger Fankhauser shows that the Reformed people have turned back on themselves by their insistence that works are necessary as evidence of genuine saving faith. They are the ones who have thrown works back into the salvation equation, not Free Grace theology. Roger says Free Grace theology "places the entire process of salvation, security, assurance, and motivation for service at the feet of Jesus." As such, the believer's only responsibility is faith, whether for initial salvation or as a basis for daily living and serving. But Christ does motivate us to faithfulness in our walk by rewards to be dispensed after His return at the Judgment Seat of Christ. However, even for the believer that loses his way and does not persevere faithfully to the end of his life, God won't let go of him. Only this kind of gospel is greater than all our sin.

Finally, Jody Dillow uses his keen analytical skills to set forth "Five Pillars of Free Grace Theology." He takes us through the journey of his own pilgrimage from his days as an unbeliever, then a moderate Calvinist, and finally a Free Grace theologian. He explains how and why his conversion to Free Grace theology took eight years. He was researching. His own self-honesty forced him to admit that many of his explanations of various challenging passages on salvation had been forced and were without evidence in the Scriptures themselves. After years of research the dots began to connect, slowly at first, and then in a rush. Suddenly everything fit. The Scriptures were coherent after all. The contradictions in his Reformed theology did not have to be explained away as mysteries. God and His ways with men began to make sense for the first time. He found greater peace for himself and greater confidence than ever in God and the Scriptures. For him Free Grace theology magnified the gospel in a way he had never known.

So, whatever your theological persuasion, if you are an evangelical Christian, then you owe it to yourself to read this brief exploration into the gospel through the lenses of some Free Grace theologians. You might be surprised. It might answer some questions that have been nagging at you for years.

Free Grace Is Returning to Scripture as Our Sole Authority

By Jeremy Edmondson

Introduction

It is hard to picture the scene. Imagine the purest feeling that has ever come over you coupled with the smell of fear. Envision a newfound burst of freedom, a sense that a long sought-after journey had just reached its destination, and yet a new one was just beginning. Imagine seeing something with unadulterated eyes within the Scriptures for the first time, even though you had read the passages time and time again. As I looked at the words, I processed them slowly. "For God so loved the world…" That's plain; God loves everyone. "…that He gave His only begotten son…" His love for everyone motivated Him to give Jesus for everyone. "That whoever believes in Him will not perish…" By having faith in God's Son, I will not experience eternal separation from God. "But has everlasting life…" By believing, I am given eternal, forever life.

The lights went on!

I had spent the better part of seven years understanding the Bible through the lens of many authors' and preachers' interpretations which were based on Reformed Calvinism and many of the creeds that came out of the Reformation. I just assumed that this is how I ought to study the Scriptures. If a scholar said it, I believed it. It had to be true because of his arguments and acumen. Then one day a dear friend asked me a jarring question: "Have you ever thought about reading the Bible and simply taking it for what it says rather than looking to another person to tell you what it means?" This was an absurd idea, thinking that I could believe what the Bible plainly says as true without consulting my bookshelf and delving into several sermons in order to come to the correct interpretation. What was most unsettling was that I realized that for seven years I had not simply read the Bible for what it says. When I first came to Christ, all I did was read the Bible. But it was when I was introduced to commentaries that my Bible study took the passenger seat so that other men could drive my spiritual growth. When I processed John 3:16 for the first time, I realized that these men, the ones that I revered and defended, the ones that I admired and coveted, had driven my spiritual life into a ditch.

I turned to look at my bookshelf, and I blurted out, "You are all wrong!"

Stephen Mansfield, writing on the life of the Guinness Family and Arthur Guinness' tenth child, Captain John Grattan Guinness, who had failed at many things during the early years of his adult life only to be renewed in his later years, writes:

> We tend to forget that there are second acts possible in the lives of most men, that an unchangeable fixity does not always rule human affairs. Many a man who has come to late middle age with despair and disillusionment has found—perhaps in love or work or devotion to a cause—the meaning or fulfillment that eluded him earlier in life.[1]

I thank the Lord Jesus for this second act permitted to me by His infinite grace which led me to consider the Scriptures in context rather than pining after the popular dead theologians of the day.

The Scriptures serve as a higher authority than that which is commonly or popularly accepted as orthodoxy. Many within evangelicalism have appealed to the Reformation, led by John Calvin and Martin Luther, as the standard of orthodoxy with which to measure and judge one's beliefs. Any conclusion that deviates from this tradition is found to be anathema in the mainstream, no matter how biblical that conclusion is. Hence the dire need for Free Grace Theology, for it alone returns to the Scriptures as the sole authority for the doctrines that it espouses. My hope is that an honest examination of the evidence provided would convince the reader of the dangers of holding the Reformation up as the standard for truth and that it would sufficiently demonstrate that the conclusions held within the Free Grace movement are biblical.

---

[1] Stephen Mansfield, *The Search for God and Guinness: A Biography of the Beer that Changed the World* (Nashville: Thomas Nelson, 2009), p. 165.

The Exaltation of the Reformation

The Reformation was undoubtedly a momentous time in Church history. Milton Terry clarifies the contents of this transitional period:

> With the Reformation of the sixteenth century the mind of Germany and of other European states broke away from the ignorance and superstition of the Middle Ages, the Holy Scriptures were appealed to as the written revelation of God, containing all things necessary to salvation, and the doctrine of justification by faith was magnified against priestly absolution and the saving meritoriousness of works.[2]

This shift in focus has been summarized in this way: "one result of the Reformation was the substitution of an infallible Bible for an infallible Church,"[3] (from which we have the cry *"sola Scriptura"*—"by Scripture alone"). This stands as the reason why every person in the free world can hold a copy of the Scriptures in his or her hands, and for that, Christians should be grateful. But one is not fully aware of the ramifications of such a movement until time has passed, doctrines are developed, and the aftermath can be surveyed in light of the Word of God.

It must be stated that the Reformation was just that—a reformation. This was the reforming of a dominant Catholic hierarchy, which had permeated the entire government. The movement allowed for certain aspects to carry over into this new ecclesiastical entity. The Reformation was not a complete separation from Catholic dogma, but showed itself to be different mainly in the quest for the reestablishment of the doctrine of justification by faith alone (cf. Rom 3:24). The goal of the Reformation was to point Christianity back to the Scriptures. The noble intentions of the Reformers called for the Bible as the supreme authority for believers everywhere. For this we rejoice! But if the Reformation and its resulting creeds are exalted to the standard of measuring orthodoxy, does it not defeat the very purpose for which it was intended?

The Reformation Was Led by Men, Thus It Was Fallible

In this great movement of history, the Bible and its place of authority over one's beliefs were elevated anew, held for the first time in opposition

---

[2] Milton S. Terry, *Biblical Hermeneutics: A Treatise on the Interpretation of the Old and New Testaments* (Grand Rapids: Zondervan, 1980), p. 673.

[3] Henry S. Curr, "The Inerrancy of the Bible," *Bibliotheca Sacra* 99 (1942): 221.

to the church that previously served as its guardian. However, the doctrines of the Reformers quickly became the center of attention. Hamilton
writes, "The Reformation was intended to establish the recognition of the
Scriptures as the final authority in matters of faith and practice, yet it has
been the case too often that men's stated interpretations of the Scriptures
have had more rigid adherence given them than the original Testimony
itself."[4] At the center of the Reformation stood Martin Luther and John
Calvin (among others) whose desire for the truth to ring true throughout
Europe should not be questioned. Anyone who follows his convictions
does so with a sincere drive. However, since it was a movement led by
men, we must necessarily conclude that this movement cannot be anything other than fallible, regardless of the good that would come out of
it. This fact led the Reformers to carry into their convictions firmly-held
Catholic beliefs not found within the Scriptures.

Infant Water Baptism

One of the most recognizable carry-overs that deviates from the
Scriptures is the Reformers' acceptance of infant water baptism. Water
baptism, scripturally understood, is an act of identification or association with someone. This is seen in Christ's baptism which identified
Him with God the Father in perfect obedience (righteousness, Matt
3:13-17), or in John the Baptist's baptism of repentance which prepared
people to believe in the One to come, namely the Lord Jesus Christ
(Mark 1:4; Acts 19:3-4), by calling them to the confession of their sins
(Mark 1:5). However, infant water baptism was a cherished sacrament
in the Reformation, and by many was considered a means of grace.[5] It is

---

[4] Alan H. Hamilton, "The Doctrine of Infant Salvation," *Bibliotheca Sacra* 102 (1945): 101.

[5] A means of grace is a method of obtaining additional grace beyond that of initial faith in Christ.
The difficulty with this concept is that it assumes that the Christian is lacking something in
Christ or that the death of Christ was not sufficient in providing all that the believer needs.
This is in contradiction to the truth found in 2 Pet 1:3-4, "His divine power has granted to us
all things that pertain to life and godliness, through the knowledge of him who called us to his
own glory and excellence, by which he has granted to us his precious and very great promises,
so that through them you may become partakers of the divine nature, having escaped from the
corruption that is in the world because of sinful desire." To clarify, Reformed theologian Louis
Berkhof writes about infant baptism as a means of grace, stating: "But baptism is more than
a sign and seal; it is as such also a means of grace. According to Reformed theology it is not,
as the Roman Catholics claim, the means of initiating the work of grace in the heart, but it is
a means for the strengthening of it or, as it is often expressed, for the increase of grace. This
gives rise to a rather difficult question in connection with infant baptism. It can readily be seen
how baptism can strengthen the work of faith in the adult recipient, but it is not so apparent
how it can operate as a means of grace in the case of children who are entirely unconscious
of the significance of baptism and cannot yet exercise faith. The difficulty with which we are

said that Luther held that "sacraments could generate faith; and hence baptism could generate faith in an infant."[6] Olson records that Luther "insisted that in order for a sacrament to be efficacious in strengthening faith, faith must be present."[7] This reasoning finds great friction in that not only is it not found in the Scriptures, which tell us plainly that "faith comes from hearing, and hearing through the word of Christ" (Rom 10:17), but also that infants are not of a conscious state to exercise faith, so no faith would be present in the infant from which he or she could benefit. In addition, Luther's understanding that the sacraments could generate faith contradicts Scripture, which requires faith to already be present in the expression of the sacraments. Luther's strongly held convictions find no scriptural support and are abounding with inconsistencies. One should be wary of accepting these convictions.

---

confronted here naturally does not exist for the small number of Reformed scholars who deny that baptism merely strengthens an antecedent condition of grace, and claim that it 'is a means for the impartation of grace in a specific form, and for the specific end of our regeneration and ingrafting in Christ.' All the others must, of course, face the problem. Luther also wrestled with that problem. He made the efficacy of baptism dependent on the faith of the recipient: but when he reflected on the fact that infants cannot exercise faith, he was inclined to believe that God by His prevenient grace wrought an incipient faith in them through baptism; and, finally, he referred the problem to the doctors of the Church. Reformed theologians solve the problem by calling attention to three things, which may be regarded as alternatives, but may also be combined. (1) It is possible to proceed on the assumption (not the certain knowledge) that the children offered for baptism are regenerated and are therefore in possession of the *semen fidei* (the seed of faith); and to hold that God through baptism in some mystical way, which we do not understand, strengthens this seed of faith in the child. (2) Attention may also be called to the fact that the operation of baptism as a means of grace is not necessarily limited to the moment of its administration any more than that of the Lord's Supper is limited to the time of its celebration. It may in that very moment serve in some mysterious way to increase the grace of God in the heart, if present, but may also be instrumental in augmenting faith later on, when the significance of baptism is clearly understood. This is clearly taught in both the Belgic and the Westminster Confession (3) Again, it may be pointed out, as has been done by some theologians (e.g. Dabney and Vos) that infant baptism is also a means of grace for the parents who present their child for baptism. It serves to strengthen their faith in the promises of God to work in them the assurance that the child for whom they stand sponsors has a right of property in the covenant of grace, and to strengthen in them the sense of responsibility for the Christian education of their child." (Louis Berkhof, *Systematic Theology* [Grand Rapids, MI: Eerdmans, 1938], pp. 641-42). Berkhof admits the difficulty in seeing how this could be true in relation to infant baptism. He admits that infants cannot exercise faith, but concludes that infant water baptism may implant a "seed of faith" in the infant. It is important to observe that 1) Those who hold to Reformed theology do not deny infant baptism as a practice that they adhere to, and 2) they must only refer to its workings in philosophical conversation because Scripture does not support this practice, nor is any reference to Scripture cited in Berkhof's explanation. This should alarm the reader to the acceptance of a plainly unbiblical practice as something that provides additional grace without scriptural support.

[6] Alister E. McGrath, *Reformation Thought: An Introduction* (Grand Rapids: Baker Book House Co., 1995), p. 179.

[7] Roger E. Olson, *The Story of Christian Theology: Twenty Centuries of Tradition and Reform* (Downers Grove, IL: IVP Academic, 1999), p. 393.

Ulrich Zwingli, the Swiss Reformer, also held fast to infant water baptism, but his reasoning differed from that of Luther, believing that "sacraments demonstrated allegiance to and membership of a community; hence baptism demonstrated that an infant belonged to a community,"[8] but again, even agreeing with this basic definition (one's identification with Christ) does not warrant that infants, who are not of the mental capacity to hear and respond to the gospel in faith (Rom 10:17; Eph 1:13), should be baptized. Search the Scriptures as you may, but this practice simply cannot be found.

The Lord's Table

A second carry-over from Catholic ideology is the Reformation's understanding of the Lord's Table, also known as the Eucharist. Luther differed slightly from the teachings of Roman Catholicism, still affirming some varied presence of the Lord Jesus' body in the bread and cup, taking Jesus' words "Take, eat; this is my body," and "Drink of it, all of you, for this is my blood of the covenant, which is poured out for many for the forgiveness of sins" (Matt 26:26-28) in a literal fashion, despite Jesus' offering literal bread and literal wine to His disciples. Caner unfolds this subtle difference, writing, "Luther denied the doctrine of Transubstantiation, rejecting any molecular change of the elements. Consubstantiation, a term never employed by Luther, is used to explain his view that the body and blood are present 'in, with, and under' the bread and wine."[9] Subtle as this difference may be, it is still far from scriptural.

Olson relates Zwingli's disagreement with Luther's view: "Luther's first error…was believing that any external thing—whether water in baptism or bread in Eucharist—can actually convey grace or faith." To do so would mean that a person's works would be necessary for salvation. He continues unfolding Zwingli's opinion, stating, "Luther erred by teaching that Christ's body is in the sacrament. For the Swiss Reformer, the two Lutheran claims amount to idolatry and christological heresy."[10] Holding fast to the Scriptures, one would have to agree with this conclusion, for the Lord's Table is never understood in the Scriptures to contain the body and blood of Jesus (a view derived from an erroneous interpretation of John 6:51, 53-58 that fails to consider the context of John 6:47-50).

---

[8] McGrath, *Reformation Thought*, p. 179.

[9] Emir Caner, "Balthasar Hubmaier and His Theological Participation in the Reformation: Ecclesiology and Soteriology," *Faith and Mission* Vol. 21, no. 1 (2003): 42.

[10] Olson, *The Story of Christian Theology*, p. 406.

In thinking through the logical implications of Luther's consubstantia-tion, one would be sacrificing Christ repeatedly every time the sacrament occurred. This conclusion speaks against the once-for-all nature of Jesus' propitiating work on the cross for the sins of the world. Paul writes, "For the death he died he died to sin, once for all, but the life he lives he lives to God" (Rom 6:10), agreeing with the author of Hebrews who writes, "He has no need, like those high priests, to offer sacrifices daily, first for his own sins and then for those of the people, since he did this once for all when he offered up himself" (Heb 7:27).

Penance/Repentance

A third carry-over concerns the subject of *repentance* and its close asso-ciation with the Catholic doctrine of penance. For the Roman Catholic Church, the sacrament of penance was a multi-faceted experience:

> The fourth sacrament is penance, of which as it were the matter consists of the actions of the penitent which are in three parts. The first of these is contrition of heart, which consists of sorrow for sin committed and the intention not to sin in the future. The second is oral confession, whereby the sinner confesses to the priest all the sins he remembers in their entirety. The third is satisfaction for sins according to the judgment of the priest, which is mainly achieved by prayer, fasting and almsdeeds.[11]

One can easily see that there is a definite sense of subjectivism involved along with a resolve to do better next time. Confession to a man is included, as well as a payment that must be rendered to essentially atone for the sin committed.

The Reformation maintained aspects of this doctrine, calling for its des-ignation as *repentance*. Calvin regarded *repentance* as "A real conversion of our life unto God, proceeding from sincere and serious fear of God; and consisting in the mortification of our flesh and the old man, and the quickening of the Spirit."[12] This view persists today within Reformed the-ology, which claims its heritage directly from the Reformers. For exam-ple, Wayne Grudem writes, "Repentance is a heartfelt sorrow for sin, a renouncing of it, and a sincere commitment to forsake it and walk in

---

[11] *The Teaching of the Catholic Church*, edited by Karl Rahner, S. J. (Staten Island, New York: Alba, 1967), p. 307, quoted in Enns, *The Moody Handbook of Theology*, p. 535.

[12] John Calvin, *Institutes of the Christian Religion* (Bellingham, WA: Logos Bible Software, 1997), iii, 3, 5.

obedience to Christ."[13] Comparing Grudem's definition to the Catholic teaching of the first step of penance, one sees striking similarities. However, it would seem that this was not always the case regarding the progression from Reformation to Reformed Theology. The idea of an emotional center was foreign to the Reformation's understanding. So where did the emotional, penance element come from?

Berkhof notes this distortion, tracing its origins to the translation of the Bible from Greek into Latin, which is known as the *Vulgate*. He writes:

> [T]he Church gradually lost sight of the original meaning of *metanoia*. In Latin theology Lactantius rendered it *"resipiscentia,"* a becoming-wise-again, as if the word were derived from *meta* and *anoia*, and denoted a return from madness or folly. The majority of Latin writers, however, preferred to render it *"poenitentia,"* a word that denotes the sorrow and regret which follows when one has made a mistake or has committed an error of any kind. This word passed into the Vulgate as the rendering of *metanoia*, and, under the influence of the Vulgate, the English translators rendered the Greek word by "repentance," thus stressing the emotional element and making *metanoia* equivalent to *metameleia*.[14]

Thus Berkhof, a prominent stalwart within Reformed theology, sees the emotional, penance association as foreign to the Scriptures.

Calvin adamantly held to a second aspect of repentance. Namely, that it could only occur after one has had faith in Christ and never before. He shows this in his *Institutes of the Christian Religion*:

> Those who think that repentance precedes faith instead of flowing from, or being produced by it, as the fruit by the tree, have never understood its nature, and are moved to adopt that view on very insufficient grounds.[15]

The appendix of this work will explain the various views of repentance held within Free Grace theology, but it is worth noting that repentance is clearly seen in Scripture as something that can occur before one's

---

[13] Wayne Grudem, *Systematic Theology: An Introduction to Biblical Doctrine* (Grand Rapids: Zondervan, 1994), p. 713.

[14] Berkhof, *Systematic Theology*, p. 481.

[15] John Calvin, *Institutes*, iii, 3, 1.

conversion as seen in John the Baptist's call of repentance to the Jews in Matt 3:2-3 stating:

> "Repent, for the kingdom of heaven is at hand." For this is he who was spoken of by the prophet Isaiah when he said, "The voice of one crying in the wilderness: 'Prepare the way of the Lord; make his paths straight.'"

However, with the response of John's disciples when they met Paul in Acts 19, we see that it is possible to repent and still not be a saved person. This passage reads:

> And it happened that while Apollos was at Corinth, Paul passed through the inland country and came to Ephesus. There he found some disciples. And he said to them, "Did you receive the Holy Spirit when you believed?" And they said, "No, we have not even heard that there is a Holy Spirit." And he said, "Into what then were you baptized?" They said, "Into John's baptism." And Paul said, "John baptized with the baptism of repentance, telling the people to believe in the one who was to come after him, that is, Jesus" (Acts 19:1-4).

From Paul's comments to these disciples, it is plain that belief and repentance are two separate things. There is no mention of sorrow or a promise to walk obediently with Christ. Also of note is that Matt 3:8 and Luke 3:8 both record the command of John the Baptist to the Pharisees that they are to "bear fruits in keeping with repentance." The Pharisees were obviously unregenerate in John's eyes (Matt 3:7; Luke 3:7), yet they are called to "bear fruit in keeping with repentance," which is an extension (separate act) from repentance. Again, there is no mention of sorrow or promises to pursue a holy walk.

Considering these three areas, we see that some doctrines that were deeply held during the Reformation are little more than extensions of what was already accepted within the Roman Catholic Church. These practices were carried on without regard to their validity in the Scriptures. Even with the best of intentions, the conviction of the Reformers in these three areas took precedence over the Word of God and served to shackle the gospel that they were so desperately trying to free.

A Reformation of Violence

Many people leading the Reformation sought to use the force of government to squash dissent. The mandatory enforcement of Reformation doctrine in some areas went as far as demanding obedience in the daily living of ordinary, unbelieving people. This is mainly due to the unbiblical goal pursued by John Calvin in seeking to turn Geneva into a spiritual utopia, using novel understandings of the Scriptures to reinforce his actions. These were not private events but are well recorded in history.

> A measure of legalism became apparent in Geneva, as the consistory put the lives of church members under continuous review and applied discipline to offenders. Church attendance was compulsory. Eating fish on Fridays was forbidden, as were attendance at theaters, dancing, card playing, and criticism of pastors. All heretical teaching was deemed subversive and subject to penalties under criminal law. Flagrant infractions could lead to banishment, imprisonment, and in extreme cases, death. Judicial torture was common procedure.[16]

Luther saw that the Church's responsibility pertained to the mind while the State pertained to the body.[17] The grip of religion on the State continued in Calvin's dominance over Geneva, which at the time was considered a normal outgrowth of all that religious institutions stood for and was not considered as reprehensible as it is today.

Biblically speaking, Calvin's ideology regarding government is heavily contrasted with that of the Apostle Paul who calls for believers to be submissive to their God-ordained authorities (Rom 13:1-7), without using the name of Christ to sway those authorities. In the case of Michael Servetus, who held the doctrine of the Trinity in question and was executed for it under Calvin's watch in 1553, Calvin wrote:

> Servetus lately wrote to me, and coupled with his letter a long volume of his delirious fancies, with the Thrasonic boast, that I should see something astonishing and unheard of. He takes it upon him to come hither, if it be agreeable to me. But I am unwilling to pledge my word for his safety, for if he shall come, I shall never permit him to depart alive, provided my authority be of any avail.[18]

---

[16] James Edward McGoldrick, "Introducing John Calvin: The Reformer's Preparation," *Reformation and Revival* Vol. 10, no. 4 (2001): 21.

[17] See William A. Mueller, *Church and State in Luther and Calvin* (Nashville: Broadman Press, 1954), pp. 28-31.

[18] Letter from Calvin to Farel, February 13, 1546, in John Calvin, *Letters of John Calvin* (Edinburgh: The Banner of Truth Trust, 1980), p. 82, cited from Laurence M. Vance, *The Other Side of Calvinism* (Orlando, FL: Vance Publications, 2001), p. 92.

Approving of the death of those who disagree on matters of faith is a principle of the world. In Scripture, one who stumbles is to be approached humbly with the hopes of being restored to sound thinking and living according to the Word of God (Matt 18:15-17a; Gal 6:1). Those who persisted in sin or who held false doctrines were cast out of the fellowship and disassociated from the church, thus being allowed to continue in their sin, which may indeed lead to death (Matt 18:17b; Rom 16:17; 1 Cor 5:1-5; 2 Thess 3:14). Enforcing or approving of their death was not an option. A movement that has opted for such measures cannot be upheld as an infallible standard.

Faith in Question

The greatest difference between Free Grace theology and Reformation theology concerns the nature of faith and what is or is not encompassed in its definition. The greatest rediscovery in all of Christian history is accredited to Martin Luther's study and contemplation regarding faith and what it means to be "justified by faith alone." Are these understandings in line with the Scriptures? An examination is necessary.

The Reformation's Definition of *Faith*

Since the Reformation was a reforming of the Catholic system and not an exclusive return to Scripture, Luther's understanding of faith and the doctrine of justification by faith alone carried some Catholic influence. Describing this, Jaroslav Pelikan writes:

> When speaking about justification by faith alone, moreover, it was essential that the "alone" not be understood as excluding the word of God and the sacraments, for these were the means by which faith was created. So inextricable a part of the doctrine of justification were the sacraments that when the Anabaptists rejected the orthodox view of baptism or when Zwingli rejected the orthodox view of the Eucharist, Luther maintained that, to be consistent, they could not possibly stand correctly on the central question of justification or on any other doctrine, although he was willing to concede that one could be saved by hearing the word of God even from such

a source. But the sacraments were so vital that whoever erred on them, "in even one point," was to be avoided.[19]

This is a frightening conviction to say the least. While many today understand the Reformation's mantra that one is "justified by faith alone, but the faith that justifies is never alone" as stating that works will always accompany faith, Luther's understanding is pregnant with the Eucharist (Lord's Supper) and baptism (be it infant or otherwise), both being works that are required by Luther in order to bring about faith unto salvation. Thus in Luther's view, justification by faith alone is not really alone in any sense of the word.

Another glimpse of the Reformation's definition of faith can be seen in the Westminster Confession, a confession that is considered to be the hallmark of Reformed Theology. It reads:

> Those whom God effectually calleth, He also freely justifieth: (Rom. 8:30, Rom. 3:24) not by infusing righteousness into them, but by pardoning their sins, and by accounting and accepting their persons as righteous: not for any thing wrought in them, or done by them, but for Christ's sake alone: not by imputing faith itself, the act of believing, or any other evangelical obedience to them, as their righteousness; but by imputing the obedience and satisfaction of Christ unto them, (Rom. 4:5–8, 2 Cor. 5:19, 21, Rom. 3:22, 24–25, 27–28, Tit. 3:5, 7, Eph. 1:7, Jer. 23:6, 1 Cor. 1:30–31, Rom. 5:17–19) they receiving and resting on Him and His righteousness by faith; which faith they have not of themselves; it is the gift of God. (Acts 10:44, Gal. 2:16, Phil. 3:9, Acts 13:38–39, Eph. 2:7–8).[20]

This definition explains that the Westminster divines considered *faith* to be "the gift of God." This explanation draws a concern.

Despite being a long-held belief of the Reformation and Reformed theology,[21] justifying faith is not a gift from God. This statement may seem alarming, but it is quite biblical, and most emphatically so from a

---

[19] Jaroslav Pelikan, *Reformation of Church and Dogma (1300-1700)*, The Christian Tradition: A History of the Development of Doctrine, Vol. 4 (Chicago: The University of Chicago Press, 1985), p. 178.

[20] *The Westminster Confession of Faith* (Oak Harbor, WA: Logos Research Systems, Inc., 1996), 11.1.

[21] See Calvin, *Institutes*, iii, 1, 4; R. C. Sproul, *What Is Faith?* The Crucial Questions Series, Vol. 8 (Lake Mary, Florida: Reformation Trust Publishing, 2010), pp. 57-58; Robert Peterson and Michael Williams, *Why I Am not an Arminian* (Downers Grove: InterVarsity Press, 2004), p. 130.

grammatical standpoint. It is essential to let the Bible shape our theology rather than bringing a theology or assumption to the text. When this happens, all one does is come to biblically unsupportable conclusions that reinforce a system that is derived from men and not from God. We are all responsible to persistently pursue God in the Scriptures and ask humbly for the leading of the Holy Spirit and wisdom in discernment. This cannot be stressed too strongly.

The idea that faith is a gift of God comes from a misreading of Eph 2:8-9: "For by grace you have been saved through faith. And *this* is not your own doing; it is the gift of God, not a result of works, so that no one may boast" (emphasis added).

Reading this passage in English, one could easily conclude that *faith* (and *grace* for that matter) is "the gift of God." Grammatically, this is impossible, hence the emphasized word *this* in the quoted passage above. First, a brief explanation of the context of this passage.

In Eph 2:1, the Apostle Paul writes that everyone, at one time, was "dead in...trespasses and sins." Reformation theology has concluded that one being dead *spiritually* is the same as being dead *physically*. They then argue that just as a corpse can do nothing to reach out or respond unless it is first made alive, so one who is spiritually dead "in trespasses and sins" cannot reach out or respond to God. The first issue with this illustration is that the word *dead* has the meaning of "separated," not unable. In addition, physical deadness and spiritual deadness are separate issues. Just because someone ceases to breathe does not mean that he ceases to exist. Otherwise, something horrific like the lake of fire (Rev 20:11-15) or infinitely beautiful like the new earth (Rev 21:1) would have no consequence in this earthly life, because the next (after) life would not be a reality. Another point to consider is just as a physically dead person cannot respond or reach out, he also cannot sin thus he cannot be held responsible for his sins. Hopefully, the point is clear.

In Eph 2:5, Paul again touches upon his statement in Eph 2:1 to show the great measure of mercy that God has shown to us. Even while we were all dead, God made us alive. Our spiritually dead state is rectified by God's doing. It is God alone who gives life. No one who holds to the Scriptures, especially those within Free Grace theology, would deny this glorious truth.

With this in mind, Eph 2:8-9 comes back to the forefront. The instance of the word *this* in "and this is not your own doing" (Eph 2:8) has been used to conclude that God gives the dead individual faith as a gift.

However, a consideration of the grammatical structure quickly puts this assumption to rest. Richard Beal and Earl Radmacher write, "A rule of Greek grammar is that a demonstrative pronoun should agree with the gender of its antecedent."[22] The ESV uses the translation, "and this" to translate *kai touto*, while other translations use, "and that," both serving as the demonstrative pronoun under consideration. The gender of this pronoun must be in agreement with the gender of its antecedent, thus, faith cannot be the gift of God. So, what is the demonstrative pronoun referring to?

To simplify this explanation, Anthony Badger writes:

> Put as simply as possible, in the phrase *through faith* (διὰ πίστεως [πίστις, εως]) *faith* is a *feminine* noun but the word *that* (τοῦτο [οὗτος, αὕτη, τοῦτο = this]) is a demonstrative *neuter* pronoun. Because of the necessity in Greek for the demonstrative pronoun to match its antecedent in gender the "*that* not of yourselves, it is the *gift* of God" could not refer to the word *faith* which is in the *feminine* gender. Further, the word *gift* (δῶρον, ου) is a *neuter* as well. The *gift* is *neuter* just like the demonstrative pronoun *that*, but neither the term *gift* nor the term *that* matches the *feminine* gender of the term *faith*. So, one must conclude that the *gift* doesn't refer to *faith*, but most naturally refers to salvation or eternal life received through faith.[23]

Greek scholar A.T. Robertson agrees with this understanding, concluding that the pronoun refers "to the act of being saved by grace conditioned on faith on our part. Paul shows that salvation does not have its source [*ex humōn*], out of you) [*sic*] in men, but from God. Besides, it is God's gift [*dōron*] and not the result of our work."[24] Daniel Wallace, considered one of today's foremost authorities in Koine Greek, explains that "τουτο [*touto*] refers to the concept of a grace-by-faith salvation. As we have seen, τουτο [*touto*] regularly takes a conceptual antecedent. Whether faith is seen as a gift here or anywhere else in the NT is not addressed by this."[25]

---

[22] R.S. Beal, Jr. and Earl D. Radmacher, *Ephesians: Life and Love in Christ* (Chino Valley, AZ: One World Press, 2012), p. 85.

[23] Anthony B. Badger, *Confronting Calvinism: A Free Grace Refutation and Biblical Resolution of Radical Reformed Soteriology*, (n.p./n.d.), pp. 81-82.

[24] A.T. Robertson, *Word Pictures in the New Testament* (Nashville: Broadman Press, 1933), Eph 2:8.

[25] Daniel B. Wallace, *Greek Grammar Beyond the Basics: An Exegetical Syntax of the New Testament* (Grand Rapids: Zondervan Publishing, 1996), p. 335. Wallace goes on in the footnote attached to the quote to address the idea of faith as a gift. He writes, "On an exegetical level, I am inclined to agree with Lincoln that 'in Paul's thinking faith can never be viewed as a meritorious

These Greek scholars affirm that salvation is the gift of God, not faith. The idea that faith is "the gift of God" finds no grammatical support. The importance of this fact cannot be overstated, especially in light of the faulty notion that God gives faith as a gift only to those whom He wishes to redeem, something that the Scriptures simply do not teach.

Therefore, "the gift of God" is properly understood as God's provision of salvation, and the sole condition for accepting this provision of salvation is faith. Anything else added to Christ as the object of faith decimates the saving power of the gospel message. Anything required other than simple faith in Him elevates the promises, commitments, creeds of man, or whatever else it may be, to the level of co-savior. The fact that Paul states that it is "not your own doing" makes it clear that we bring nothing to this gift of God's provision of salvation; we are simply receiving as fact the work that has already been done for us.

One simply cannot theologically conclude what he cannot prove through careful exegesis.

The Free Grace Definition of Faith

So what is the Free Grace definition of *faith* and how is it different from the Reformers' definition of *faith*? In the Scriptures, *faith* always means "a conviction, a belief" (with certainty) that something is true. This understanding is without prejudice to matters involving the full scope of salvation truth (justification, sanctification, or glorification), for the *faith* involved is always the same.[26] This is exactly what the definition of *faith* in Heb 11:1 communicates: "Now faith is the assurance of things hoped for, the conviction of things not seen." Lenski has translated this verse as, "Now faith is firm confidence in things hoped for, conviction regarding things not seen."[27]

---

work because in connection with justification he always contrasts faith with works of the law (cf. Gal 2:16; 3:2-5, 9, 10; Rom 3:27, 28)' (A.T. Lincoln, *Ephesians* [WBC] 111). If faith is not meritorious, but instead the *reception* of the gift of salvation, then it is not a gift per se. Such a view does not preclude the notion that for faith to save, the Spirit of God must initiate the conversion process."

[26] "Faith is the key principle by which we are to relate to God, whether it is in receiving His grace for salvation or receiving His grace for Christian living." (Charles C. Bing, *Grace, Salvation, and Discipleship: How to Understand Some Difficult Bible Passages* [The Woodlands, TX: Grace Theology Press, 2015], p. 51).

[27] R. C. H. Lenski, *The Interpretation of the Epistle to the Hebrews and of the Epistle of James* (Columbus, OH: Lutheran Book Concern, 1938), p. 373.

This definition of faith as "assurance" and "conviction" should not be understood as two separate halves that make up the whole of faith. Both "assurance" and "conviction" are one and the same. The word translated "assurance" is *hupostasis* meaning, "guarantee of ownership/entitlement, *title deed*."[28] The word for "conviction" is *elenchos* which means "the evidence, normally based on argument or discussion, as to the truth or reality of something."[29] This word can mean "proof" (HCSB) but seems best rendered as "conviction."[30] It is clear that the two are synonymous, as Vincent affirms, "υποστασις [*hupostasis*] and ελεγχος [*elenchos*] are not two distinct and independent conceptions, in which case καί [*kai*] and would have been added."[31] Thus, we see that faith is both confidence and conviction. To define *faith* as including works or obedience is to say something other than what is clearly stated in Heb 11:1.

The Word of God is Central to Faith

In contrast with the Reformation teaching that faith is a gift from God, Free Grace theology holds that "The Word of God is the agency by which faith is generated."[32] What saves a person is hearing and believing the Word of God regarding Christ Jesus. The Apostle Paul writes, "faith comes from hearing, and hearing through the word of Christ" (Rom 10:17). The Apostle Peter also concurs: "you have been born again, not of perishable seed but of imperishable, through the living and abiding word of God" (1 Pet 1:23). James elevates this truth, stating, "Of his own will he brought us forth by the word of truth" (Jas 1:18). The Lord Jesus had much to say about the importance of the Word of God as the agency by which faith is generated, but most pertinent is John 5:24, "Truly, truly, I say to you, whoever hears my word and believes him who sent me has eternal life. He does not come into judgment, but has passed from death to life." The emphasis on the Word of God as the agency by which faith is generated cannot be ignored.

---

[28] Walter Bauer, *A Greek-English Lexicon of the New Testament and Other Early Christian Literature*, rev. and ed. Fredrick Wm. Danker, 3rd ed. (Chicago: University of Chicago Press, 2000), s.v. *hupōstasis*.

[29] Johannes P. Louw and Eugene Albert Nida, *Greek-English Lexicon of the New Testament: Based on Semantic Domains* (New York: United Bible Societies, 1996), s.v. *elenchos*.

[30] See Robertson, *Word Pictures*, Heb 11:1.

[31] Marvin Richardson Vincent, *Word Studies in the New Testament* (New York: Charles Scribner's Sons, 1887), 4:510.

[32] Lewis Sperry Chafer, *Systematic Theology* (Dallas: Dallas Seminary Press, 1983), 1:121.

Free Grace also finds no evidence for faith as a gift when the Old Testament teaching on faith is considered. In the Old Testament, Abram's conversation with God regarding the promise of children in his old age is the chief example that Scripture puts forth to communicate the nature of faith. After inquiring of the Lord regarding His promise made in Gen 12:1-3 for offspring, and the perceived slackness of the fulfillment of that promise, God replies, "Look toward heaven, and number the stars, if you are able to number them." Then He said to Abram, "So shall your offspring be" (Gen 15:5). We are then told, "And he believed the LORD, and he counted it to him as righteousness" (Gen 15:6). This sets the foundation for how we should understand faith as presented in the Scriptures. Abram's response teaches us that faith comes from hearing God's Word, and it is obvious that he was convinced by what God had said (Heb 11:1). We know this because we are told that he was declared righteous (justified) upon believing. The Scriptures record no time in Abram's life when he was given faith as a gift. The gift of faith is a foreign concept as far as the Bible is concerned.[33]

God Draws the Dead Through the Cross

Some may respond that a person who is spiritually dead cannot believe. They would advocate that the gift of faith must be given to the person after he has been regenerated (born again) by God.[34] Then he can believe and be saved. This view was held by both Calvin and Luther. Enns writes:

> Because of man's condition of total depravity, Calvin disavowed the idea of a free will; that was forfeited through the fall. He

---

[33] In Gal 5:22, the ESV records "faithfulness" as a gift of the Spirit. It is clear from the surrounding context that this is not speaking to one's justification but to fruit that the Spirit produces in the Christian's life as he submits to the Word of God. We must remember, this is the Spirit's fruit through the believer, not the believer's fruit, for the flesh profits nothing (John 6:63; Rom 8:8).

[34] R.C. Sproul writes, "So we are reborn, we hear the Word of God, we believe, we are justified, we are adopted, and we are sealed by the Holy Spirit. All of these things are part of the order of God's work of redemption in us." (Sproul, *What Is Faith?* p. 58). Calvin and Luther held that unregenerate people are unable to respond to God when they hear the gospel. This means that these people have no hope of salvation since they were not born again and given the gift of faith by God. The idea that one is unable to respond to God is not something that is found in the Bible. In Acts 10:1-2, Cornelius, who was not a believer in Jesus Christ (Acts 10:44-48), was considered a "devout man who feared God" and who "prayed continually to God" (Acts 10:2). If the gift of faith theory were true, the unregenerate person's sealed destiny in the lake of fire is God's fault because He withheld his only chance of being saved. The gifted faith view is logical within Calvinism, but is purely philosophical and certainly not biblical. René Lopez writes, "Nowhere does Scripture teach the inability of individuals to respond to God's drawing. In fact one finds just the opposite. For example Jesus said, 'If anyone is thirsty, let him come to Me and drink' (John 7:37). And 'the Spirit and the bride say "Come"' (Rev. 22:17). Otherwise

taught that the will is bound, unable to move in any direction except toward evil. Yet Calvin taught that man is held responsible for his sin because he sins out of his own will and not by any outward compulsion. Moreover, although man's reason is impaired, man can discern between good and evil; therefore man is responsible for "not willing the good but the bad."

The corollary doctrine of total depravity is predestination, which Luther, Calvin, and Zwingli all affirmed. Because man was unable to make a positive move toward God as a result of his depravity, it was necessary for God to predestine certain ones to salvation.[35]

But is this what the Scriptures teach?

A common verse used to defend this Reformation perspective is John 6:44: "No one can come to me unless the Father who sent me draws him." With this verse, many would consider the matter a closed case, at least until the context is considered. Jesus states in the next verse, "Everyone who has heard and learned from the Father comes to me" (John 6:45b), meaning that the Word about Christ has been shared and those who understand the Word come to Christ. Later in the book, Jesus elaborates on the Father's drawing of people when He states, "And I, when I am lifted up from the earth, will draw all people to myself" (John 12:32). In order to eliminate any confusion as to Jesus' meaning, John provides an editorial note in the next verse, stating, "He said this to show by what kind of death he was going to die" (John 12:33; see also John 3:14-15). So it is the event of the crucifixion of Christ that has paid for the sins of the world and has made it possible for the world to come to Christ in faith when people hear and understand His Word. This account testifies that the Word of God is the agency that generates faith in the unregenerate person.

Depravity in Relation to Faith

Let it not be imagined that Free Grace does not believe in the total depravity of mankind. We wholeheartedly affirm Paul's distress in Romans 3:10-18 that none seek after God and that none are righteous, that all have turned aside and that no one does good. Let it be understood that man cannot do anything of merit in regard to his salvation in any way,

---

how could God blame people for not acknowledging Him or believing in Christ (John 5:40)?" (Rene A. Lopez, "Is Faith a Gift from God or a Human Exercise?" *Bibliotheca Sacra* 164:655 [2007]: 262).

[35] Paul Enns, *The Moody Handbook of Theology* (Chicago: Moody, 1989, 2008), p. 448.

shape, or form. However, Free Grace does not hold that mankind's total depravity is total inability. Man can respond in faith to the Lord when he is drawn, and what draws him is the message about Christ's crucifixion (John 6:44-45).

The reason for man's depravity (not inability) is explained by the Apostle Paul who writes in Romans, "Therefore, just as sin came into the world through one man, and death through sin, and so death spread to all men because all sinned" (Rom 5:12). He goes on to state:

> For if, because of one man's trespass, death reigned through that one man, much more will *those who receive the abundance of grace and the free gift of righteousness* reign in life through the one man Jesus Christ. Therefore, as one trespass led to condemnation for all men, so *one act of righteousness leads to justification and life for all men.* For as by the one man's disobedience the many were made sinners, so by the one man's obedience the many will be made righteous (Rom 5:17-20, emphasis added).

Paul is clear that all are sinners and that all need righteousness. Only those "who receive the abundance of grace and the free gift of righteousness" will be given "justification and life." Paul is clear that "all" are eligible for this gift, not just some. It is only those who believe in Christ that will be justified and given the free gift of eternal life.

This concept is also clear in Eph 1:13 which gives a biblical order of salvation (*ordo salutis*). Paul writes, "In him you also, when you heard the word of truth, the gospel of your salvation, and believed in him, were sealed with the promised Holy Spirit." Notice the order that Paul gives his readers regarding how they were saved. First, they "heard the word of truth." This "word" is the "gospel of your salvation." Next, they believed in Christ, having heard the word about Him. Finally, Paul notes that they were "sealed with the promised Holy Spirit," having been given eternal life and are now eternally secure thanks to Christ's finished work on the cross.

Free Grace affirms that mankind is totally depraved, unable to do anything to save himself, but we do not hold that mankind is unable to believe when presented the gospel. The Word of God is the agency by which faith is generated. Faith in Christ is man's response to the gospel presentation.

What About Works?

An often-asked question involves the place of works regarding one's salvation. John Calvin held to the idea that one's justification was progressive and not an instantaneous act. He writes:

> But though it is by mercy alone that God admits his people to life, yet as *he leads them into possession of it by the course of good works*, that he may complete his work in them in the order which he has destined (emphasis added).[36]

Such a comment mixes justification and sanctification, thus necessitating good works. The emphasis on the necessity of accompanying works in Reformation theology has been well documented.[37] It is falsely assumed that those who hold to the Free Grace position minimize the importance of works in the Christian life and have in turn been accused of encouraging sin. This is a misguided conclusion that has failed to consider the positions of those in the Free Grace camp and is often touted by those who have not carefully studied the Judgment Seat of Christ in the Scriptures (Rom 14:10-12; 1 Cor 3:10-15; 2 Cor 5:10).

It is not that those who advocate Free Grace deny the presence of works in a believer's life. However, Free Grace theology holds that works are not a sufficient means of determining someone's born again state.[38] Such a conclusion gets the biblical result of faith in Jesus Christ wrong, making the equation:

$$\text{Faith} + \text{Jesus} = \text{Works}$$

Reformation thought has made works a necessary result of faith. Whether works are required at the beginning or are expected at the end, they are

---

[36] Calvin, *Institutes*, iii, 18, 1.

[37] See Wayne Grudem, *"Free Grace" Theology: 5 Ways it Diminishes the Gospel*, pp. 28-38; Calvin, *Institutes*, iii, 14, 21; Alan P. Stanley, *Did Jesus Teach Salvation by Works? The Role of Works in Salvation in the Synoptic Gospels* (Eugene, OR: Pickwick Publishers, 2006), pp. 52-56; Thomas R. Schreiner and Ardel B. Caneday, *The Race Set Before Us: A Biblical Theology of Perseverance and Assurance* (Downers Grove, IL: InterVarsity, 2001), pp. 47-52.

[38] Zane Hodges notes the significance of this issue: "We must add that there is no need to quarrel with the Reformers' view that where there is justifying faith, works will undoubtedly exist too. This is a reasonable assumption for any Christian unless he has been converted on his death bed! But it is quite wrong to claim that a life of dedicated obedience is guaranteed by regeneration, or even that such works as there are must be visible to a human observer. God alone may be able to detect the fruits of regeneration in some of His children. What is wrong in lordship thought is that a life of good works is made the basis of assurance, so that the believer's eyes are distracted from the sufficiency of Christ and His Cross to meet his eternal need. Instead, his eyes are focused on himself. The Reformers understood that there was no assurance in that kind of process at all." (Zane C. Hodges, *Absolutely Free: A Biblical Reply to Lordship Salvation*, [Grand Rapids, MI: Zondervan, 1989], p. 215).

still rendered an indispensable part of justification. This leads to no other conclusion than that man's performance is necessary for his justification to be complete.[39] "Everyone prefers the feeling of being able to do something to be saved," states Radmacher. "And once the door is open to this kind of thinking, the whole emphasis shifts away from salvation as a gift of God."[40] This error is why a biblical understanding of justification is crucial.

Free Grace considers the justification equation to be:

Faith + Jesus = Eternal Life

This equation allows for justification to be a completed event, with the sinner declared righteous by God because of the work of Jesus Christ and perfectly secure in this declaration with the promise of eternal life. The sinner has done nothing to earn this standing and most certainly can do nothing to overturn the free declaration of God toward him. It is from this divinely secured position that the believer in Christ can now look to the Word of God and the indwelling Spirit of God to work together in changing him from the inside out (Jas 1:21). With one's position secured, his practice becomes a product of his completed state and not a part of it.

Those who advocate for the necessity of works will find complications with the Apostle Paul's argument in Rom 2:14 which states, "For when Gentiles, who do not have the law, by nature do what the law requires, they are a law to themselves, even though they do not have the law." Mounce provides clarification on Paul's point:

> Whenever Gentiles by natural instinct did what the law required, they demonstrated the existence of a guiding principle within themselves. Twice in v. 14 Paul stressed that non-Jewish people had no specific knowledge of the Mosaic legislation. They did "not have the law." Yet in certain cases they did instinctively the kinds of things required by the Jewish law (e.g., they cared for the sick and elderly, showed kindness to strangers). They were, as Paul put it, "a law for themselves." That does not mean that

---

[39] The argument for this line of thinking is that the good works that are evident in the Christians' lives are done by God through them, thus demonstrating the authenticity of their salvation. The problem with this explanation is that a person's good works are never perfect. If these are works done by God through the person, why does Paul exhort his Christian readers to "be steadfast, immovable, always abounding in the work of the Lord, knowing that in the Lord your labor is not in vain" (1 Cor 15:58)? Such an exhortation is unnecessary if God is already doing good works through the person. The only other conclusion is that God is satisfied with doing less than perfect works through believers, or that works are not a verification of one's justification, but are seen when the believer is convicted by the Word of God and by trusting what has been read, moves forward in faith so as to walk in the Spirit (Rom 8:13). The latter is the biblical solution.

[40] Earl D. Radmacher, "What Is Faith?" *Understanding Christian Theology*, Charles R. Swindoll and Roy B. Zuck eds., (Nashville: Thomas Nelson Publishers, 2003), p. 866.

law was irrelevant in their case but that their conduct revealed a general knowledge of God's requirements for a principled and virtuous life. Not only did God reveal himself to them in nature (Rom 1:19–20) but he created them with a sense of moral obligation. This moral impetus encouraged a conduct that at many points overlapped what was taught in the laws of God given to Israel.[41]

Gentiles, in their natural state, that is, their unregenerate state,[42] were found to be doing works that complied with the Law because of what was "instinctive" for them to do. This means that all of mankind has an inherent understanding of right and wrong, actions and deeds that would be found to be in line with the Law of Moses. Thus, works cannot be a means of gauging one's regenerate state when Paul has clearly pointed out that unregenerate Gentiles were keeping the Law (doing works that were in line with the Law) about which they knew nothing.

Reflecting upon one's works diminishes the eternal nature of the saving work of Christ on the cross, since Christians, being in the flesh, can have both good and bad works throughout their lifetime. Consequently, if one has believed in Christ but upon examining his works, he concludes that he is not saved, what does this say about the power of Christ's sacrifice to keep him? Was Jesus not able to save him completely? After all, faith is the only condition put forward in the Scriptures by which one receives eternal life. Judging one's salvation based upon his works in this life has some serious implications that serve to diminish the power of the Cross while elevating the one who judges to the position of sovereign.[43]

---

[41] Robert H. Mounce, *Romans, The New American Commentary*, Vol. 27 (Nashville: Broadman & Holman, 1995), pp. 94–95.

[42] I believe that Paul in Romans 2:12–3:20 is speaking about unregenerate Jews and Gentiles. It would be unusual for Paul to advocate the Jews keeping the Law for justification in 2:13 if they were believers in Christ (cf. 6:14; 7:6; 10:4). His point is that if someone could keep the Law and obey perfectly, he or she would be considered righteous. This conclusion allows Paul to make the statement in 3:19 that all are guilty under the Law and in 3:20 that the Law serves to expose sin.

[43] This was something that John Calvin understood, even though it makes his requirement for works a contradiction in his theology. He writes, "When we so examine ourselves, however, it is not to see whether our holiness, our works, or the fruit of the Spirit in our lives warrant assurance of salvation. Rather, it is to determine that such assurance rests on the proper foundation of God's mercy in Christ. Because of the phenomenon of temporary faith, we see that our feelings are an unreliable test of our standing with God. Therefore, if we are to be sure of our salvation, we must always direct our gaze to Christ, in whose face we see the love of God for us fully displayed." (Charles M. Bell, *Calvin and Scottish Theology: The Doctrine of Assurance* [Edinburgh: Handsel Press, 1985], p. 30, quoted from Joseph C. Dillow, *The Reign of the Servant Kings: A Study of Eternal Security and the Final Significance of Man* [Monument, CO: Paniym Group, 2011], p. 250).

The Christian life is not about reforming the flesh, but seeking to trust in God's Word and relying upon the indwelling Spirit of God to change us from the inside out (Jas 1:21). Christians have had bad days, weeks, months, and even years. In some cases, the Church is to blame for these periods of carnality within a believer's life. Many churches have failed to disciple believers (Matt 28:18-20) so as to grow them from infants into maturity (1 Pet 2:2). Others have judged them in their infantile stages for their worldly behavior, driving them from the Church before they had been given the chance to grow. Either way, introspection does not win and is not a sufficient barometer for gauging one's Christianity.

For Free Grace, Justification is Crucial

An unsaved person's acceptance by God is only possible if he or she has the very righteousness of God. It alone is perfection. The only alternative would be that the person is perfect himself. Works, if anything, only serve to further condemn a person. Acceptance before God is not something that can be earned. Paul writes of this in Rom 3:20, "For by works of the law no human being will be justified in his sight, since through the law comes knowledge of sin." For human works to earn any merit with God is impossible. God's righteous standard, as found in the Law of Moses, clearly lists the expectations of God's perfection. It is through this Law that the knowledge of sin comes about.[44]

Justification is the central tenet of the Reformation; every believer should be grateful that Luther rediscovered it after many years of lying buried under the heap of Roman Catholic hierarchy. An unsaved person's only hope for salvation is that he or she would be "justified in His sight" (Rom 3:20). *Justification* as biblically understood "is the forensic *declaration* that the Christian is righteous, rather than the process by which he or she is *made* righteous. It involves a change in *status* rather than in *nature*."[45] This definition and its ramifications deserve careful consideration.

---

[44] Some have advocated that since the Law was given to the Jews only, it is only the Jews who have broken the Law. This understanding contradicts what Paul is plainly teaching in Romans 3:20 and would require that the truths about being justified "freely by His grace" that follow would pertain only to the Jews as well. Those who have not broken the Law have no need to be justified, yet we are all sinners who have broken God's Law, and it is only by measuring our actions against God's Law that we can determine what sin is and what it isn't. Therefore, the Law serves as the written standard of perfection that considers the whole world accountable for its actions (Rom 3:19).

[45] Alister McGrath, *Justification by Faith* (Grand Rapids: Academie Books, 1988), p. 61. Emphasis in original.

Declared Righteous or Made Righteous?

One is declared righteous by God at the moment that he or she responds in faith to the gospel of Jesus Christ (Rom 10:17; Eph 1:13). McGrath's contrast is important, since the concept of one being *made righteous* as a concise definition of justification is a Catholic doctrine that promotes an improvement of the flesh by keeping certain criteria. How one understands justification depends on how one views the Reformers' insistence that faith be accompanied by works as the necessary evidence of genuine conversion. As argued above, does this insistence not thrust the very meaning of *justification* out of the realm of forensics and into the flesh, from the realm of Protestant back into Catholic? Such thinking is an additional example of another concept that has carried over from the Roman Catholic system into the outworkings of Reformation theology.

Concerning the biblical meaning of justification, Moule elaborates:

> Justification means properly no less than this, the being received by Him as if we had not grieved Him. It is not only, [*sic*] the being forgiven by Him. We do indeed as sinners most urgently need forgiveness, the remission of our sins, the putting away of the holy vengeance of God upon our rebellion. But we need more. We need the voice which says, not merely, you may go; you are let off your penalty; but, you may come; you are welcomed into My presence and fellowship.[46]

This understanding is central to Free Grace. While one can never be *made righteous* while in the flesh, one can be *declared righteous* by the Creator of all things. It is how one is "declared righteous" that consumes Paul as he writes:

> But now the righteousness of God has been manifested apart from the law, although the Law and the Prophets bear witness to it—the righteousness of God through faith in Jesus Christ for all who believe (Rom 3:21-22a).

God's righteousness has been made known apart from works. This is the righteousness that the unbeliever desperately needs. By stating that "the Law and the Prophets bear witness to it," Paul is showing that the Old Testament had advocated this truth all along (Gen 15:6). This righteousness is God's perfection, made available to every person on Earth (Rom 5:12-19). In order to eliminate any confusion as to how a lawbreaker can

---

[46] H. C. G. Moule, "Justification by Faith," in *The Fundamentals: A Testimony of Truth*, ed., R. A. Torrey (1917; repr., Grand Rapids: Baker Books, 2008), 2:145.

be accepted before God, Paul states that this perfect righteousness comes "through faith [*pistis*] in Jesus Christ for all who believe [*pisteuō*]."

Note that Jesus Christ alone has made this a possibility and that there is a complete absence of any works required by the one needing God's righteousness. The terms used are *faith* and *believe* with the Greek provided in italics for the reader so that the similarity in language can be seen. Paul puts forth no expectation of works. God's perfect righteousness can be counted in the person's favor through faith alone (by itself), in the Lord Jesus Christ alone (by Himself).

Paul continues:

> For there is no distinction: for all have sinned and fall short of the glory of God, and are justified by his grace as a gift, through the redemption that is in Christ Jesus, whom God put forward as a propitiation by his blood, to be received by faith (Rom 3:22b-25).

Paul's words are clear: Everyone is a lawbreaker ("sinner," cf. Rom 3:19-20). But just as all are guilty of sin and cannot save themselves, so anyone can be justified before God by personal faith alone in Jesus Christ alone. This salvation is an act of grace, which God has put forward as a gift. Grace is God's unearned favor on an infinitely ill-deserving people. God's act of grace is that His Son Jesus has died on the cross for the sins of the world (John 1:29; Heb 2:9; 1 John 2:2), paying for them with His blood, and making the redemption of mankind possible.

All of this can be received by one way only, by faith alone (by itself) in Jesus Christ alone (by Himself). Justification was never meant to be authenticated by works. If this were so, Paul would have included such expectations within this portion of Scripture. Yet, Paul remains silent. To require anything else in receiving a gift of God's grace, even if it is an expectation of moral, ethical, or mental improvement, is to make this gift a transaction. For Paul, the focus in justification is on the redeeming work of the Lord Jesus Christ, not on the improved behavior of the new believer.

Moral Improvement?

Now, simply by reading Paul's words in Romans 3, would one conclude that the concept of justification carried any moral improvement in its meaning? Certainly not! Imagine the misconstrued emphasis that would overshadow the glorious truth that sinners, who are of flesh which profits nothing and adds nothing (John 6:63; Rom 8:8), are accepted by Almighty God based on the merits of Christ. Moule gives a sublime understanding:

> Take a ready illustration to the same effect from Scripture, and from a passage not of doctrine, but of public Israelite law: "If there be a controversy between men, and they come unto judgment, that the judges may judge them, then they shall justify the righteous and condemn the wicked" (*Deuteronomy* 25:1). Here it is obvious that the question is not one of moral improvement. The judges are not to make the righteous man better. They are to vindicate his position as satisfactory to the law.[47]

Neither the forthcoming works of man nor consideration of his moral performance has any place in the realm of justification. To do so is to supplant Christ Jesus as the sole advocate, sacrifice, and substitute for the sins of man. To place them in that realm is to necessitate human works in order to complete justification. To do so is to say that Christ's death is insufficient. To do so is heresy.

Shouldn't Christians Be Doing Something?

What is damaging to the Reformers' demand for works-evidence is Paul's silence about any mandate upon the believer throughout the rest of Romans 3…and Romans 4…and Romans 5…and it is not until chapter 6 that Paul issues an imperative, calling on believers to consider themselves "dead to sin and alive to God in Christ Jesus" (Rom 6:11). Since this is the nearest work to Paul's unfolding of the glorious truths of justification by faith alone in Jesus Christ alone, those who hold to works as a necessary evidence of justification must either conclude that those who do not consider themselves dead to sin are not truly saved, or must come to believe that one is declared righteous by God because he has been credited with the very righteousness of God because of the sufficient work of Jesus Christ on the cross. The latter is the only means of one's acceptance before God.

For Paul to call believers to consider themselves "dead to sin and alive to God in Christ Jesus" (Rom 6:11) is to call on them to think according to the reality of their standing before the Most High God. No works are implied. Verifying someone's justification becomes increasingly difficult by this first imperative, seeing that it is something that deals with one's

---

[47] *Ibid.*, p. 143.

thinking about himself, and not an action to be performed. While people will live, operate, and make decisions and choices differently after considering themselves in this way, the Christian who does not consider himself dead to sin will not have (first) the mental victory that will lead to (second) the physical outworking for all to see. This is why Paul later states:

> Let not sin therefore reign in your mortal body, to make you obey its passions. Do not present your members to sin as instruments for unrighteousness, but present yourselves to God as those who have been brought from death to life, and your members to God as instruments for righteousness. For sin will have no dominion over you, since you are not under law but under grace (Rom 6:12-14).

The Christian who fails to think this way has not shown himself to be unsaved, but disobedient, and in doing so, will suffer the consequences of participating in sinful acts because he is not thinking of himself as dead to sin. He neglects the fact that Christ has died for his sins and has freely justified him before the Father.

A Cause for Concern

With these major differences between Reformation theology and Free Grace, the concern is not with the inerrancy, infallibility, inspiration, or revelation of the Scriptures. Both sides wholly affirm their perfection in the original autographs. However, there is a concern regarding what the excessive elevation of the Reformation as a standard of orthodoxy says concerning the sufficiency of the Scriptures. In explaining what is meant by *sufficiency*, Gilley writes:

> When I speak of the sufficiency of the Bible, I mean that it alone is adequate to train us in godliness. Only the Word reveals God's truth for living. On the negative side, this naturally implies that nothing needs to be added to the Scriptures for us to know truth and live godly lives. Therefore, when anything, whether it is man's wisdom, personal experience, pragmatism, tradition, or direct revelation, is touted as a means of accomplishing these things, then biblical sufficiency has been denied. By this definition we find the conservative Christian landscape literally covered with those who claim to believe

in the authority of Scripture, yet in practice deny it by their extra-biblical sources of obtaining truth and guidance.[48]

This is precisely the problem under consideration. Free Grace theology holds the Holy Scriptures of the Old and New Testament to be all-sufficient for doctrine and practice, needing no additional commentary or creed. Free Grace magnifies the gospel in that the Scriptures are allowed to speak authoritatively above the voices of Luther and Calvin (or the wisdom of any other men), showing God's Word to be sufficient for all of life, as well as to impart life (Rom 10:17).

To consider the firmly held beliefs of the Reformers as the judge and jury of doctrinal matters sidesteps (whether intentionally or unintentionally) the Scriptures as the sole authority for how one should formulate his understanding of God, Jesus, salvation, creation, the Church, Israel, and a host of other doctrines. Not only so, but it also introduces an additional aspect and expectation of Christian conduct, since a standard for right thinking (orthodoxy) must necessarily give way to right living (orthopraxy). The undue elevation of the Reformation overshadows the Word of God, covering up its liberating truth.

Conclusion

We see that a demand for good works in the Christian's life serves the Reformed understanding that faith is a gift imparted to the individual, so that his salvation can be assumed to be genuine, at least until the moment when bad works become observable. This thinking, and the entire ideology with which the Reformers interpret the Bible, is rooted in the Catholic system of works salvation, which demands evidence of one's conversion and provides no assurance of salvation. All of this has been neatly packaged under the title of "historic Protestantism," and is commonly touted as a revolutionary break from the trappings of Rome's Church. With the evidence supplied, I believe that you will agree that this separation is not complete.

Most troubling is that such an elevation of the Reformers and their doctrines has placed them in a position of authority. This again demonstrates the carryover mentality within areas of Evangelicalism that cannot seem to shake the trappings of early Catholic dogma, for Catholics consider the Scriptures to be authoritative, but hold that the Catholic Church holds

---

[48] Gary E. Gilley, *Is That You Lord? Hearing the Voice of the Lord: A Biblical Perspective* (Grand Rapids: EP Books, 2014), p. 105.

a greater authority when the Word of God speaks in a direction that is against their dogma. In the same way, when one considers the Reformation as the standard of orthodoxy, it becomes an authority over and against the Word of God.

A sincere question has been addressed to Free Grace leaders: "Where in the entire history of mainstream Reformation Protestantism...did you ever find the idea that justification by faith alone means that it is faith by itself, without anything accompanying it?"[49] Examining the evidence, the answer would confidently be, "we did not get this from the Protestant Reformation, but from the Holy Scriptures." Free Grace Theology, therefore, magnifies the gospel because it magnifies the Scriptures as its sole authority.

---

[49] Wayne Grudem, "Salvation without Repentance from Sin: A Critique of the Free Grace Gospel," https://www.youtube.com/watch?v=lfi168XDUX8, 13:45-14:06. Last accessed June 20th, 2016. See also, Grudem, "Free Grace" Theology, pp. 32-33.

FREE GRACE TEACHES US TO TURN FROM SINS

By Editor

Introduction

Victor Hugo's classic *Les Misérables* tells the story of a peasant named Jean Valjean, who escapes after having been imprisoned for nineteen years for stealing a loaf of bread. He finds no help for some time, since he is a fugitive. Then one evening, he knocks on the door of the Bishop of Digne, who has compassion for him. The Bishop gives him shelter and food, treating him with the dignity that he has not been given in many years, if ever. This touching exchange illustrates the enormity of such a small thing:

> The Bishop, who was sitting close to him, gently touched his hand. "You could not help telling me who you were. This is not my house; it is the house of Jesus Christ. This door does not demand of him who enters whether he has a name, but whether he has a grief. You suffer, you are hungry and thirsty; you are welcome. And do not thank me; do not say that I receive you in my house. No one is at home here, except the man who needs a refuge. I say to you, who are passing by, that you are much more at home here than I am myself. Everything here is yours. What need have I to know your name? Besides, before you told me you had one which I knew."

> The man opened his eyes in astonishment.

> "Really? You knew what I was called?"

> "Yes," replied the Bishop, "you are called my brother."

"Stop, Monsieur le Curé," exclaimed the man. "I was very hungry when I entered here; but you are so good, that I no longer know what has happened to me."[1]

But Valjean repays his great kindness by stealing his silverware. At this point, it might seem as though grace has no power to change a man's heart. He has been shown grace but abused it. This only shows that people can and do abuse grace.

But after Valjean has been arrested for stealing, the Bishop covers for him, saying that the silverware was a gift (Did he not say, "Everything here is yours"?) and rebukes Valjean for forgetting to take the silver candlesticks:

> "Ah! Here you are!" he exclaimed, looking at Jean Valjean. "I am glad to see you. Well, but how is this? I gave you the candlesticks too, which are of silver like the rest, and for which you can certainly get two hundred francs. Why did you not carry them away with your forks and spoons?"

Valjean deserves punishment, but he receives blessing. He has done nothing to earn the grace he receives. It is given freely. The reach of the Bishop's grace toward Jean Valjean astonished him. And as Valjean stands trembling before the Bishop, the Bishop says, "Jean Valjean, my brother, you no longer belong to evil, but to good."

Valjean went on to become an honest and trustworthy businessman who treats his employees with respect and kindness and becomes so well known as a righteous man that he is elected mayor. A dose of grace was abused, but limitless grace transformed this man. Nineteen years of hard labor and imprisonment as punishment for stealing bread could not soften Jean Valjean's heart, but one evening and morning of true grace did.

Limitless grace is what God has shown us, and this grace is powerful in transforming us as well. This is what the Apostle Paul was discussing when he wrote to his dear friend Titus:

> For the grace of God has appeared, bringing salvation for all people, training us to renounce ungodliness and worldly passions, and to live self-controlled, upright, and godly lives in the present age, waiting for our blessed hope, the appearing of the glory of our great God and Savior Jesus Christ, who gave himself for us to redeem us from all lawlessness and to purify

---

[1] Victor Hugo, *Les Misérables*, Isabel F. Hapgood, trans., electronic ed. Available online at: https://www.gutenberg.org/files/135/135-h/135-h.htm. Last accessed June 16th, 2016.

for himself a people for his own possession who are zealous for good works. (Titus 2:11-14)

Grace, unmerited favor, is what trains us to live godly lives.

What Is Sin?

Sins Are Not Only External

For us to fully understand why it is God's free grace that calls us to turn from sins, we need to have an accurate understanding of what sins are. Sins are not limited to external things like adultery and drunkenness, but include internal thoughts, desires, and motivations. Coveting, that is, inappropriately desiring what rightly belongs to another, is one example of sin that may not have any outward expression at all. I can covet my neighbor's car and never say a word or do anything about it, yet I have still sinned.

Making it clear that sins include internal things is one of the purposes of the Sermon on the Mount in which Jesus said:

> "Beware of practicing your righteousness before other people in order to be seen by them, for then you will have no reward from your Father who is in heaven. Thus, when you give to the needy, sound no trumpet before you, as the hypocrites do in the synagogues and in the streets, that they may be praised by others. Truly, I say to you, they have received their reward. But when you give to the needy, do not let your left hand know what your right hand is doing, so that your giving may be in secret. And your Father who sees in secret will reward you. And when you pray, you must not be like the hypocrites. For they love to stand and pray in the synagogues and at the street corners, that they may be seen by others. Truly, I say to you, they have received their reward. But when you pray, go into your room and shut the door and pray to your Father who is in secret. And your Father who sees in secret will reward you." (Matt 6:1-6)

Thus, God sees into the heart and takes motives into consideration. The one who practices righteousness with the wrong motive is sinning and will not be rewarded for it.

Taking this a step further, sin also includes anything that is not from faith (Rom 14:23). Something that may not be sinful for one person, like expressing a Christian liberty, may be sinful for another because he lacks faith. Even things we would all consider good, like singing to the Lord, giving to the poor, or studying the Bible, can be sinful when not arising out of faith. That means that if we do good works to try to earn God's grace or because we are afraid He will withdraw His grace we are sinning, because we are doubting Christ's promises to us (John 5:24; 6:47-51; 10:27-30; 11:25-26).

Finally, when we lack love, nothing we do can please the Lord:

> If I speak in the tongues of men and of angels, but have not love, I am a noisy gong or a clanging cymbal. And if I have prophetic powers, and understand all mysteries and all knowledge, and if I have all faith, so as to remove mountains, but have not love, I am nothing. If I give away all I have, and if I deliver up my body to be burned, but have not love, I gain nothing. (1 Cor 13:1-3)

Even the greatest feats of righteousness, like self-sacrifice, are nothing if love isn't present.

Indwelling Sin

Further complicating our war against sin's influence is that sin itself, a force which drives us to commit sins, lives within our bodies. Speaking of an experience he had as a Christian,[2] the Apostle Paul wrote:

> Did that which is good [the Law], then, bring death to me? By no means! It was sin, producing death in me through what is good, in order that sin might be shown to be sin, and through the commandment might become sinful beyond measure. For we know that the law is spiritual, but I am of the flesh, sold under sin. For I do not understand my own actions. For I do not do what I want, but I do the very thing I hate. Now if I do what I do not want, I agree with the law, that it is good. So now

---

[2] Romans 7:9 says, "I was once alive apart from the law, but when the commandment came, sin came alive and I died." The way Paul uses the term *alive* and related terms in Romans has to do with experiencing the power of the resurrection life of Christ, and with it, freedom from sin's domination (see Rom 6:6-11; 8:2). The Apostle would never call someone who was not resurrected to new life with Christ "alive," and, since he was a Pharisee and a strict observer of the Law from the beginning of his life until he came to faith in Christ (Phil 3:5-6), he cannot say of his pre-Christian life that he was "apart from the law."

it is no longer I who do it, but sin that dwells within me. For I know that nothing good dwells in me, that is, in my flesh. For I have the desire to do what is right, but not the ability to carry it out. For I do not do the good I want, but the evil I do not want is what I keep on doing. Now if I do what I do not want, it is no longer I who do it, but sin that dwells within me. So I find it to be a law that when I want to do right, evil lies close at hand. For I delight in the law of God, in my inner being, but I see in my members another law waging war against the law of my mind and making me captive to the law of sin that dwells in my members. (Rom 7:13-23)

This passage tells the story of a believer who desires to do good but consistently fails. He tries to control sin through observance of the Law, but sin would not allow it. He chose coveting as his example, because while people may be able through a strong will and commitment to avoid things like adultery or murder, those things have no power over internal sins like coveting.

Transformation Is Needed

Why is it significant that sin includes internal things and that it dwells within our bodies? If sin and righteousness have to do with internal thoughts, feelings, motivations, faith, and love, and if we have sin dwelling in our bodies driving us to commit sins, only a transformation from the inside out can accomplish meaningful change. Our thoughts and desires have to undergo a metamorphosis.

You may be thinking, "Yes, but a transformation automatically occurs when we are regenerated and the Holy Spirit comes to indwell us." That is true in a sense, but the transformation we need to live as God desires is something in addition to regeneration. Even as a Christian, Paul still needed deliverance from sin's power in his life: "Wretched man that I am! Who will deliver me from this body of death?" (Rom 7:24). Likewise, Paul, writing to believers in Christ (Rom 1:7, 12; 5:1), gives the imperatives, "Do not be conformed to this world, but be transformed by the renewal of your mind, that by testing you may discern what is the will of God, what is good and acceptable and perfect" (Rom 12:2). He follows this by a series of practical applications including love for one another, humility, and other things, which all depend on this transformation occurring. Regeneration makes such a transformation possible, but regeneration itself is not this transformation, or people who have already been regenerated would not still need it.

Grace Is Powerful to Effect Transformation

Ephesians 2:1-10 is a powerful passage that shows how effective grace is at preparing us for good works. These Ephesian believers had previously been dead in trespasses and sins (2:1), had walked in the will of the devil (2:2), and were wrathful by nature (2:3).[3] This is a fair description of those outside of Christ. Then, verse four begins with one of the most beloved phrases in Scripture, "But God…" As these Gentiles went about their lives serving themselves and the enemy of God, God steps in to intervene. The next four verses tell us what God did and why:

> But God, being rich in mercy, because of the great love with which he loved us, even when we were dead in our trespasses, made us alive together with Christ—by grace you have been saved—and raised us up with him and seated us with him in the heavenly places in Christ Jesus, so that in the coming ages he might show the immeasurable riches of his grace in kindness toward us in Christ Jesus. (Eph 2:4-7)

Even though we were completely without merit and living in total rebellion, God loved us. He loved us so much that He "made us alive together with Christ" and will spend eternity pouring out the "immeasurable riches of his grace in kindness toward us in Christ Jesus." This is the story of Jean Valjean and the Bishop of Digne, only immeasurably greater.

To be sure we don't miss an important point, Paul adds, "For by grace you have been saved through faith. And this is not your own doing; it is the gift of God, not a result of works, so that no one may boast" (Eph 2:8-9). God saves the one who simply believes the gospel (1 Cor 15:3-4; cf. Eph 1:13).[4] Salvation is His free gift to us.[5] Grace excludes all boasting,

---

[3] Though some have argued differently, the genitive in 2:3 translated, "[children] of wrath," is best understood as an attributive genitive rather than a genitive of purpose or direction. This is a common idiom in Hebrew culture and "children of _____" and "sons of _____" are often used to demonstrate character qualities (see Matt 5:9, 45; John 8:37-41; Eph 5:6; Col 3:6). Coupled with the phrase, "by nature," the case for the attributive genitive is strong. That is, wrath was a dominant character quality of these people prior to their salvation.

[4] The words *faith* and *believe* translate *pistis* and *pisteuō*, respectively. The root word is the same, but *faith* translates the noun form, whereas *believe* translates the verb form.

[5] Some say that *faith* is the gift in view, but this is grammatically impossible in the Greek, since *faith* is feminine and the pronoun *that* is neuter. Greek pronouns have to agree with their antecedents in number and gender. The neuter demonstrative pronoun, *touto, this*, is commonly

because we did nothing to earn His favor. What a tragedy it would be to boast in ourselves in light of this extravagant display of God's perfect love!

It is after this, after grace is freely given to the undeserving and after these believers had been made alive together with Christ, that Paul points to a greater purpose in v 10, which reads, "For we are his workmanship, created in Christ Jesus for good works, which God prepared beforehand, that we should walk in them."[6] We are created in Christ Jesus for good works. We aren't saved just to be saved, we are saved to do good works.

Grace and Humility

But it is grace that prepares us for these good works, and if we have to work to receive grace, then it wouldn't be grace at all, as Paul writes, "But if it is by grace, it is no longer on the basis of works; otherwise grace would no longer be grace" (Rom 11:6).

Grace, free grace (since there is no other kind), is essential to preparing us for the good works God has prepared for us. This is because grace leaves us no room to boast, as we saw in Eph 2:9 and as Rom 3:23-27 expresses:

> [F]or all have sinned and fall short of the glory of God, and are justified by his grace as a gift, through the redemption that is in Christ Jesus, whom God put forward as a propitiation by his blood, to be received by faith. This was to show God's righteousness, because in his divine forbearance he had passed over former sins. It was to show his righteousness at the present time, so that he might be just and the justifier of the one who has faith in Jesus. Then what becomes of our boasting? It is excluded. By what kind of law? By a law of works? No, but by the law of faith.

---

used to refer to abstract concepts (like by-grace-though-faith salvation) that are not expressed by a noun in the context.

[6] The word translated *workmanship* only occurs twice in the New Testament, once in Rom 1:20, referring to the created universe, and once here in Eph 2:10, referring to the new creation. While in extra-biblical literature and the LXX, it can refer to more mundane works in certain contexts (though, not when God is doing the work), in this instance, it is better translated *masterpiece* for two reasons. First, it better reflects the majesty of the work of God that Paul is discussing, and second, we can distinguish that it is singular (as the Greek word is), which cannot be done with the English, *workmanship*. That is, we, together, are His singular masterpiece. Verses 11-22 explain more about why we, the Body of Christ, are God's masterpiece. See NLT, ISV, OJB.

Boasting is excluded because God alone contributes to our justification; our only part is to receive a free gift through faith in Jesus. The degree to which we recognize this fact is the degree to which it will humble us. Our worth as individuals and our standing in righteousness are found in Christ alone, and we are no more deserving of grace than anyone else. Only Free Grace theology consistently and sufficiently keeps us focused on what Christ has done and not focused on ourselves.

Humility and Power to Obey

Being humbled in this way prepares us for a holy walk. This is not only because God delights in humility, but because humility will drive us "to the throne of grace, that we may receive mercy and find grace to help in time of need" (Heb 4:16). The grace in view in Heb 4:16 is grace to overcome temptation and tribulation, which we receive each time we go to Christ for help.

The prideful person thinks that he can overcome sin through his own efforts, even if he wouldn't say so openly. But as Paul recognized, there is nothing good dwelling in our flesh (Rom 7:18), but only sin (Rom 7:17, 20), and it is only by the strength of Christ's life—as we place our trust in Him—that we are able to prevail (Romans 7:24–8:6).

Humility and Love

Humility will also lead us to consider others ahead of ourselves: "Do nothing from selfish ambition or conceit, but in humility count others more significant than yourselves" (Phil 2:3). Counting others as more significant than ourselves is a good way to define *agapē* love. As Paul writes:

> Love is patient and kind; love does not envy or boast; it is not arrogant or rude. It does not insist on its own way; it is not irritable or resentful; it does not rejoice at wrongdoing, but rejoices with the truth. Love bears all things, believes all things, hopes all things, endures all things. (1 Cor 13:4-7)

Every aspect of this description of love is inseparably linked with considering others ahead of ourselves. For example, if we put ourselves first, we will never be able to be patient and kind toward our brothers, because instead of causing compassion in us, their struggles will seem like annoyances or impositions. We will envy what others have because we think we deserve it more and will be boastful, arrogant, and rude. Instead of giving deference, we will insist on our own way in everything. You see, love and humility cannot exist without each other. Even God, Who is love, demonstrates His humility in His greatest act of love, namely, that while we were yet sinners, Christ came to earth to serve, suffer, and die for us (Rom 5:8; Phil 2:5-8).

The Lord's new commandment to us is that we would love one another as He has loved us (John 13:34). There is no such thing as a Christ honoring life that is not characterized by love. And there is no such thing as love that isn't humble. For this reason, we must let grace be grace, not adding (explicitly or implicitly) a condition of works, so that we will never boast, but be humbled before the Lord Jesus Christ, our brothers and sisters in Christ, and the world.

Grace and Thankfulness

Thankfulness is a powerful motivator. The Apostle Paul represents a great example. He was, in his own estimation, the foremost of sinners (1 Tim 1:15), yet he received grace for justification and grace unto apostleship. He received this grace as a secure gift, even while he was in the midst of persecuting our Lord and Savior Jesus Christ (Acts 9; cf., Rom 5:6-8). This grace transformed him from being a Pharisee, zealously persecuting the Church and seeking *personal* advancement (Gal 1:14) to being the most tireless missionary and the most abundant laborer among the apostles (2 Cor 11:22-28), one in whom *God* was glorified (Gal 1:23-24). Grace humbled Saul of Tarsus and made him thankful. That thankfulness drove his life and ministry (Gal 2:20).

But that kind of thankfulness only comes when the recipient of a great gift is aware of what he has been given. That is, full assurance—knowing we have everlasting life—and the peace that comes with that knowledge, is what makes us thankful. But where do we get such assurance? Some say we must look within ourselves to see if we measure up over time. More than a century ago, C. H. Mackintosh expressed the scriptural answer:

> Christ, having shed His blood as a perfect atonement for sin, has taken it into the presence of God and sprinkled it there; and God's testimony assures the believer that everything is settled on his behalf.

> All the claims of justice have been fully answered; sin has been perfectly put away, so that the full tide of redeeming love may

roll down from the heart of God, along the channel which the sacrifice of Christ has opened for it.

To this truth the Holy Ghost bears witness. He ever sets forth the fact of God's estimate of the blood of Christ. He points the sinner's eye to the accomplished work of the cross. He declares that all is done; that sin has been put far away, and righteousness brought nigh — so nigh, that it is "to all them that believe." Believe what? Believe what God says, believe because He says it, not because you feel it.

Now, we are constantly prone to look at something in ourselves as necessary to form the ground of peace. We are apt to regard the work of the Spirit in us, rather than the work of Christ *for us*, as the foundation of our peace. This is a mistake. We know that the operations of the Spirit of God have their proper place in Christianity, but His work is never set forth as that on which our peace depends. The Holy Ghost did not make peace; but Christ did. The Holy Ghost is not said to be our peace; but Christ is. God did not send "preaching peace" by the Holy Ghost, but by "Jesus Christ." (Comp, Acts 10:36; Eph. 2:14, 17, Col. 1:20)[7]

Our true ground of peace is Christ's finished work on the cross—which occurred apart from us and can be objectively verified—not a subjective look at inward transformation, which can never erase the fear of death. Assurance based on the finished work of Christ is what the author of Hebrews is expressing when he writes:

Since therefore the children share in flesh and blood, he himself likewise partook of the same things, that through death he might destroy the one who has the power of death, that is, the devil, and deliver all those who through fear of death were subject to lifelong slavery. (Heb 2:14-15)

Fear of death brings slavery to sin and to the devil, not obedience to God, not thankfulness. It is deliverance from fear that rescues us from such bondage and gives us solid ground upon which we can "stand against the schemes of the devil" (Eph 6:11b). Only with this peace can we say with Paul, "Thanks be to God for his inexpressible gift!" (2 Cor 9:15).

---

[7] C. H. Mackintosh, "The True Ground of Peace," publication date unknown, available online at http://www.stempublishing.com/authors/mackintosh/Pprs/CHMPEACE.html. Emphasis in original. Last accessed, July 20th, 2016.

Our Own Recognition of Free Grace Is Necessary

In Wayne Grudem's new book, *"Free Grace" Theology: 5 Ways It Diminishes the Gospel*, to which this book is offered as a contrast, he makes a helpful analogy. He writes:

> Now it is perfectly true to say that my office door is *opened by the blue key alone* (it is the only key that works to open that door). But the blue key is *never by itself*, because I always keep it on the key ring with the yellow key (which opens the faculty office corridor), the plain key (which opens the classroom doors), and the small key (which opens the computer door at the podium where I teach). Therefore my office door is opened by the blue key alone (it is the only key that works), but the blue key that opens my office door is never alone (it is never found by itself but is always accompanied by other keys).
>
> This simple statement about my keys is parallel to the historic Reformation teaching that we are justified by faith alone (faith is the only response that God requires from us), but the faith that justifies is never alone (because it never occurs by itself…).[8]

This illustration is helpful because it leads us to the question, in keeping with the analogy: If the blue key was removed from the key ring, so that it was by itself, would it still open his office door? If the only room we needed to get into was Dr. Grudem's office, would we need the yellow key, the plain key, and the small key? And if the blue key is sufficient to open his office door, would we need to worry about being able to get into the office if any of the others were missing? Could we not look for the yellow key when we needed to open the faculty office corridor, and the plain key when we needed to open a classroom door, etc.?

This is the difference between Free Grace and non-Free Grace.[9] Free Grace teaches that anyone who has the blue key (faith), can be confident

---

[8] Grudem, *"Free Grace" Theology*, p. 38. Emphasis in original.

[9] I am using the term *non-Free Grace* instead of *Lordship Salvation* at the request of Dr. Grudem (*ibid.*, pp. 22-26). While I do believe the term *Lordship Salvation* correctly describes the views of some, Dr. Grudem is right to say that his view is not correctly characterized by the term. Dr. Grudem also uses the term *historic Protestant* to describe his view, and this would be a fair term except that it neglects to consider the historic Dispensational tradition, which is also an important movement within Protestantism, and which has always been Free Grace or Free Grace-friendly. See Grant Hawley, "Dispensationalism and Free Grace: Intimately Linked, Part 3" in *Journal of the Grace Evangelical Society* 25:48 (Spring 2012): 21-36. This article, along with the first and second installments, is being published by Dispensational Publishing House as part of a new book by the same title and will be available in December of 2016.

of his access into the office (justification and eternal life), even if he is missing the other keys (such as works, baptism, etc.).

It is an unproductive exercise to ask whether there is such a thing as a believer with absolutely no good works. That is not the distinction between Free Grace and non-Free Grace. The distinction is found in asking whether we objectively look to Christ for our assurance or subjectively look to our works for the same. The former is Free Grace; the latter is not.

But the sad fact is that in some believers, faith is closer to being *by itself* than we would like. We have to ask ourselves, what about those cases? If there are believers who don't meet our standard of good works, and there are, then it is applying the "no true Scotsman" fallacy[10] to say, "no *true* believer falls short of our standard of good works." If we do that, we have to acknowledge that God requires something more than faith to be with Him forever—He also requires an undisclosed quantity and quality of works. The end result is that we have to look to our works for assurance, which will never be able to grant assurance, except in those who are not sensitive to their own sin.

This brings us to my main point. If I look to my works for assurance, this diminishes grace's power to produce humility and thankfulness in me. How can it humble me, if I am to subjectively look to my own attainment to determine whether or not I am justified before God (cf. Rom 4:1-5)? In practicality (though not ultimately), that would make me my own judge. Likewise, if I am given a gift that I must prove worthy of to count as mine, would this not be less effective at making me thankful than if I am given the same gift freely?

I was not always a proponent of Free Grace. I once held to traditional Reformed soteriology. When I accepted Free Grace theology, I was crushed, even to weeping at what Christ had done for me and that I could truly be at peace with God, even though I was deeply undeserving of it. An enormous burden had been lifted. So, as for my own experience, Free Grace brought me low and made me thankful in a way that non-Free Grace had not.

So, in this way, it is important—even vital to a God-honoring walk with Christ—that we accept the freeness and security of the gift of grace

---

[10] "Example: Angus declares that Scotsmen do not put sugar on their porridge, to which Lachlan points out that he is a Scotsman and puts sugar on his porridge. Furious, like a true Scot, Angus yells that no true Scotsman sugars his porridge." "No True Scotsman," author unknown, available online at https://yourlogicalfallacyis.com/no-true-scotsman. Last accessed, July, 20th, 2016. This is considered a fallacy because it is intended to make a truth claim unfalsifiable.

we have been given. It is that freeness and security that make it effective to produce humility and thankfulness.

Scripture Attests to the Transforming Power of Grace

Jean Valjean's story is moving, but it is also fiction. The question arises regarding whether or not freely-given grace has the same transforming power in reality. Thankfully, we have relevant teaching on this subject in inspired, inerrant Scripture.

A visit to a Pharisee's house in Luke 7 affords Jesus an opportunity to teach on the transforming power of grace:

> One of the Pharisees asked him to eat with him, and he went into the Pharisee's house and reclined at table. And behold, a woman of the city, who was a sinner, when she learned that he was reclining at table in the Pharisee's house, brought an alabaster flask of ointment, and standing behind him at his feet, weeping, she began to wet his feet with her tears and wiped them with the hair of her head and kissed his feet and anointed them with the ointment. Now when the Pharisee who had invited him saw this, he said to himself, "If this man were a prophet, he would have known who and what sort of woman this is who is touching him, for she is a sinner." And Jesus answering said to him, "Simon, I have something to say to you." And he answered, "Say it, Teacher." "A certain moneylender had two debtors. One owed five hundred denarii, and the other fifty. When they could not pay, he cancelled the debt of both. Now which of them will love him more?" Simon answered, "The one, I suppose, for whom he cancelled the larger debt." And he said to him, "You have judged rightly." Then turning toward the woman he said to Simon, "Do you see this woman? I entered your house; you gave me no water for my feet, but she has wet my feet with her tears and wiped them with her hair. You gave me no kiss, but from the time I came in she has not ceased to kiss my feet. You did not anoint my head with oil, but she has anointed my feet with ointment. Therefore I tell you, her sins, which are many, are forgiven— for she loved much. But he who is forgiven little, loves little." (Luke 7:36-47)

The English translation is a bit misleading at the end. Jesus is making the point that the one who is first forgiven much will love more than one who is forgiven little (Luke 7:41-43), but the English translation at the end suggests that the love comes before the forgiveness. The issue is that the word translated "for" is *hoti*, which in some contexts can mean "for" or "because," looking to a cause, but can also mean, "so that," looking toward a result.[11] The context makes the translation, "so that," necessary here in Luke 7:47. Jesus is not teaching that we buy His forgiveness with great love. In fact, Jesus clarifies that the catalyst for her forgiveness was her faith (Luke 7:48-50), not her work of love. Jesus is teaching the undeniable principle (even Simon the Pharisee knew it intuitively) that the more a person, such as this woman, has been forgiven, the more she will love the One who forgave her.

By contrast, "he who is forgiven little, loves little" (Luke 7:47). The example of the older brother in the Parable of the Lost Son (Luke 15:11-30) is fitting. Though he had all the privileges of being a son of such a gracious and wealthy father, when his brother returned, he was angry at his father's rejoicing and celebrating his lost son's return. His complaint was based on the fact that he had done little that needed to be forgiven:

> "…he answered his father, 'Look, these many years I have served you, and I never disobeyed your command, yet you never gave me a young goat, that I might celebrate with my friends. But when this son of yours came, who has devoured your property with prostitutes, you killed the fattened calf for him!'" (Luke 15:29-30)

In reality, the father in this story was affording his angry son a great deal of grace and patience even in that very conversation. But in his ungratefulness, the son was not aware of the depth of grace he was being shown, since he was comparing his iniquity to that of someone else, namely his little brother, whom he would not even acknowledge as his brother ("this son of yours"). The one who thinks he has been forgiven little, loves little.

---

[11] Walter Bauer, *A Greek-English Lexicon of the New Testament and Other Early Christian Literature*, rev. and ed. Fredrick Wm. Danker, 3rd ed. (Chicago: University of Chicago Press, 2000), p. 593. See also, Daniel B. Wallace, *Greek Grammar Beyond the Basics* (Grand Rapids, MI: Zondervan, 1996), p. 677. See John 7:35 for a similar use of *hoti*.

The Judgment Seat of Christ[12]

Not only is the doctrine of the absolute freeness of the gift of everlasting life effective to produce humility, thankfulness, and love, Free Grace theology also has the added motivation of the Judgment Seat of Christ. What is the Judgment Seat of Christ? This is a common question for people to ask when they are new to the concept of Free Grace, because it is something that is not often taught outside of Free Grace circles.

The Bible teaches that every human being will face judgment for his or her works. Jesus said, "The Father judges no one, but has given all judgment to the Son (…) And he has given him authority to execute judgment, because he is the Son of Man" (John 5:22, 27). Judgment is universal in scope, and no human being will escape it, including those who believe in Jesus. Many understand this principle to mean that believers and unbelievers will be judged alongside one another at the Great White Throne Judgment (Rev 20:11-15), and that at that judgment all true believers will have enough works to prove that they were truly saved.[13] Teachers who hold this view often use the term *final judgment*. One author, referring to the Great White Throne Judgment in Rev 20:11-15, writes:

> *All* the dead are judged in view of what is written in the books. This includes believers and unbelievers, elect and non-elect. This is a judgment of all people: "I saw *the dead*, great and small" (v. 12). "*The dead* were judged" (v. 12). "The sea gave up *the dead* who were in it, Death and Hades gave up *the dead* who were in them, and they were judged" (v. 13). So believers and unbelievers face what is written in the books.[14]

But this confuses two very different judgments. The Great White Throne Judgment referenced above is a judgment for the dead, not for those who are alive with God's eternal life. Those who believe in Christ "shall never die" (John 11:26), but instead "will live forever" (John 6:51). For us who believe, when our physical bodies die, the Bible says we are "asleep" (1 Thess 4:13-15), and believers who sleep in Christ will have already been awakened from that sleep, and will have been living in new, glorified

---

[12] This section is adapted from Grant Hawley, "What Is the Judgment Seat of Christ?" in *21 Tough Questions about Grace*, Grant Hawley, ed. (Allen, TX: Bold Grace, 2014), pp. 91-97.

[13] "There will be enough evidences of grace that God will be able to make a public display of what is in the books to verify the born-again reality of those written in the book of life. No one is saved on the basis of his works. But everyone who is saved does new works." John Piper, "What Will the Final Judgment Mean for You?" Available online at http://www.desiringgod.org/articles/what-will-the-final-judgment-mean-for-you. Last accessed Nov. 21st, 2014).

[14] *Ibid.*, Emphasis in original.

bodies for over a thousand years by the time the "books" are opened in
Rev 20:11-15 (cf. Rev 20:4-6). If you believe in Jesus Christ, then you
will not be judged alongside the dead (John 5:24).

Two Judgments

There are two seats of judgment mentioned in Scripture—the *Bēma*,[15]
and the *Thronos* (throne). D. M. Panton observed: "The tribunal, before
which disciples appear, is peculiar. It is a *Bema*, not a *Thronos*; [*sic*] a judgment seat for the investigation of disciples, not a throne for the arraign-
ment of rebels."[16] The *Bēma* will occur before the Millennial Kingdom
(Matt 16:27), and the *Thronos*, the judgment for unbelievers, will occur
after the Millennium (Rev 20:7, 11-15).

The judgment that believers will face is called the Judgment Seat of
Christ, or the *Bēma*. This is what Paul was referring to when he wrote to
his fellow believers in Corinth:

> So whether we are at home or away, we make it our aim to
> please him. For we must all appear before the judgment seat
> of Christ, so that each one may receive what is due for what
> he has done in the body, whether good or evil. (2 Cor 5:9-10)

Christ will not judge believers at the *Bēma* based upon His own righteousness, or upon His own works, but the works of the believer, though
it is by His indwelling Spirit that we can do good works. This is not a
place for grace and receiving free gifts. It is a place for receiving wages
for work done. At the *Bēma*, the truth of Paul's statement, "Do not be
deceived: God is not mocked, for whatever one sows, that will he also
reap" (Gal 6:7), will be apparent.

Throughout the New Testament, the Judgment Seat of Christ takes
center stage, and references and allusions to it occur on almost every page
(one notable exception is the Gospel of John[17]). Because every book in the
New Testament—outside of the Gospel of John—was written to believers, it makes sense that each writer would be working to prepare his readers for the judgment of their life's work.

---

[15] *Bēma* is a Greek word that is often translated "judgment seat."

[16] D. M. Panton, *The Judgment Seat of Christ* (Hayesville, NC: Schoettle Publishing Co., Inc.
1984), pp. 14-15.

[17] Philemon also contains no references to the *Bēma* in its twenty-five verses.

The Judgment Seat of Christ is Not for Determining Eternal Destiny

The Judgment Seat of Christ is not to determine eternal destiny. Believers cannot enter into that kind of judgment: "Truly, truly, I say to you, whoever hears my word and believes him who sent me has eternal life. He does not come into judgment, but has passed from death to life." (John 5:24). The *Bēma* is for the determining of rewards.

In Luke 19:11-27, the Lord gives us a picture of the *Bēma* in a parable:

> As they [His disciples] heard these things, he proceeded to tell a parable, because he was near to Jerusalem, and because they supposed that the kingdom of God was to appear immediately. He said therefore, "A nobleman went into a far country to receive for himself a kingdom and then return. Calling ten of his servants, he gave them ten minas, and said to them, 'Engage in business until I come.' But his citizens hated him and sent a delegation after him, saying, 'We do not want this man to reign over us.' When he returned, having received the kingdom, he ordered these servants to whom he had given the money to be called to him, that he might know what they had gained by doing business. The first came before him, saying, 'Lord, your mina has made ten minas more.' And he said to him, 'Well done, good servant! Because you have been faithful in a very little, you shall have authority over ten cities.' And the second came, saying, 'Lord, your mina has made five minas.' And he said to him, 'And you are to be over five cities.' Then another came, saying, 'Lord, here is your mina, which I kept laid away in a handkerchief; for I was afraid of you, because you are a severe man. You take what you did not deposit, and reap what you did not sow.' He said to him, 'I will condemn you with your own words, you wicked servant! You knew that I was a severe man, taking what I did not deposit and reaping what I did not sow? Why then did you not put my money in the bank, and at my coming I might have collected it with interest?' And he said to those who stood by, 'Take the mina from him, and give it to the one who has the ten minas.' And they said to him, 'Lord, he has ten minas!' 'I tell you that to everyone who has, more will be given, but from the one who has not, even what he has will be taken away. But as for these enemies of mine, who did not want me to reign over them, bring them here and slaughter them before me.'"

In this parable, there are two broad categories of people—servants, and enemies. The king goes away to a far country to receive a kingdom, and in the meantime, his servants are each given one mina (about one fourth of a year's wages for an agricultural worker) and told to do business with it until he returns.

Upon the king's return, he speaks with each servant to find out the return on his investment. We only see three examples of these ten servants, probably because they are representative of the three main kinds of servants. There are those whose work is very fruitful, like the servant who earned ten minas with the one he was given. There are those whose service is fruitful, but not as much as it could be, like the one who earned five. And there are those who do nothing to give the king a return on his investment.

Interestingly, it was a legalistic mindset that drove the unfaithful servant to unfruitfulness. He said, "Lord, here is your mina, which I kept laid away in a handkerchief; for I was afraid of you, because you are a severe man. You take what you did not deposit, and reap what you did not sow" (19:20-21). Ironically, the truth about Christ's character is exactly the opposite. As the Lord said to the Israelites, "I gave you a land on which you had not labored and cities that you had not built, and you dwell in them. You eat the fruit of vineyards and olive orchards that you did not plant" (Josh 24:13). Even the mina this servant had to work with was a gift from the king.

But the king judges this lazy servant based upon the false standard the servant had ascribed to his king: "I will condemn you[18] with your own words" (Luke 19:22).

The minas here represent responsibility. We are each given responsibility in this life. We are enabled and charged to work, using the spiritual enablement Christ has given us, to build up the Body of Christ. If we are faithful with this small task, we will be given much more responsibility upon Christ's return. This responsibility will be in proportion to our labors now, though the reward is exceedingly generous (i.e., authority over ten cities for producing two and a half years' worth of a poor worker's wages). On the other hand, if we do nothing with what we are given, we

---

[18] *Condemn* is much too strong for the Greek word *krinō*, "I will judge" in this context. See J. H. Moulton and G. Milligan, *Vocabulary of the Greek Testament* (Peabody, MA: Hendrickson Publishers, 1930, 2004), p. 360. See also Luke 19:22 in, ASV, KJV, HCSB, NASB, NET, NIV, NKJV, NRSV, YLT.

will not receive any responsibility at that time, and even the responsibility we have now will be taken away:

> And he said to those who stood by, "Take the mina from him, and give it to the one who has the ten minas." And they said to him, "Lord, he has ten minas!" "I tell you that to everyone who has, more will be given, but from the one who has not, even what he has will be taken away." (Luke 19:24-26)

Christ will not entrust the administration of His kingdom to those who are unfaithful with what He has given them now.

But even with this picture of a negative judgment, this wicked servant is contrasted with the king's enemies: "But as for these enemies of mine, who did not want me to reign over them, bring them here and slaughter them before me" (Luke 19:27). This refers back to his citizens in 19:14 who hated him. The enemies are not even present when the servants are judged. It is after the judgment that the king says, "But as for these enemies of mine…bring them here."

So, while we will all be presented before Christ to be judged, the issue is not our eternal destiny. The issue is the determining of rewards.

The Judgment Seat of Christ Is Foundational to Free Grace Theology

The Judgment Seat of Christ is a doctrine foundational to Free Grace. Throughout the Bible, it is clear that there is a prize to be won, wages to be earned, and loss ahead if we fall away. When scholars do not give rightful place to the *Bēma*, and instead join the two separate judgments—the one for believers only and the one for unbelievers—into one, they end up with believers before the *Thronos*, being judged by their works to determine their eternal destiny. Likewise, the very real accountability we have is softened as the Judgment Seat of Christ is eliminated.

Below is a small chart of contrasts between the free gift and the prize:

The Free Gift	The Prize
For by grace you have been saved through faith. And this is not your own doing; it is the gift of God, not a result of works, so that no one may boast. (Eph 2:8-9)	For the Son of Man is going to come with his angels in the glory of his Father, and then he will repay each person according to what he has done. (Matt 16:27)

The Free Gift	The Prize
Jesus answered her, "If you knew the gift of God, and who it is that is saying to you, 'Give me a drink,' you would have asked him, and he would have given you living water." (John 4:10)	The one who conquers and who keeps my works until the end, to him I will give authority over the nations. (Rev 2:26)
He saved us, not because of works done by us in righteousness, but according to his own mercy, by the washing of regeneration and renewal of the Holy Spirit. (Titus 3:5)	Do you not know that in a race all the runners run, but only one receives the prize? So run that you may obtain it. Every athlete exercises self-control in all things. They do it to receive a perishable wreath, but we an imperishable. So I do not run aimlessly; I do not box as one beating the air. But I discipline my body and keep it under control, lest after preaching to others I myself should be disqualified. (1 Cor 9:24-27)
…and are justified by his grace as a gift, through the redemption that is in Christ Jesus. (Rom 3:24)	And let us not grow weary of doing good, for in due season we will reap, if we do not give up. (Gal 6:9)
The Spirit and the Bride say, "Come." And let the one who hears say, "Come." And let the one who is thirsty come; let the one who desires take the water of life without price. (Rev 22:17)	"Behold, I am coming soon, bringing my recompense with me, to repay each one for what he has done." (Rev 22:12)

One passage in particular discusses the gift and the prize together, clearly making a distinction:

> For we are God's fellow workers. You are God's field, God's building. According to the grace of God given to me, like a skilled master builder I laid a foundation, and someone else is building upon it. Let each one take care how he builds upon it. For no one can lay a foundation other than that which is laid, which is Jesus Christ. Now if anyone builds on the foundation with gold, silver, precious stones, wood, hay, straw—each one's work will become manifest, for the Day will disclose it, because it will be revealed by fire, and the fire will test what sort of work each one has done. If the work that anyone has built on the foundation survives, he will receive a reward. If anyone's

work is burned up, he will suffer loss, though he himself will be saved, but only as through fire. (1 Cor 3:9-15)

Thus the gift, salvation, cannot be lost, even if a believer's works are burned up. It is the *reward* that is at stake. The Greek word for "burned up" is *katakaiō*, which essentially means *to burn to the ground* or *to burn up completely*. This depicts someone whose work is entirely burned up, meaning that he receives no reward at all. "Though," Paul says, "he himself will be saved, but only as through fire" (1 Cor 3:15). The picture here is someone escaping a burning house. His house is destroyed, but he escapes with his life.

This means that even if a believer does not produce sufficient quality of works to reap a reward, his or her eternal destiny is secure. Understanding the reality of the Judgment Seat of Christ helps us keep the grace of God in perspective. We need not fear the lake of fire, but the accountability so clearly laid out in Scripture applies to us, not just to false professors. This fact is important because it means that being caught up in any sins—even those sins the church does not always take seriously—and leaving undone the works we are called to do will have a direct impact on our rewards. We cannot dismiss passages about our accountability as only applying to other people, people who aren't true believers.

A Word About Rewards

The rewards we can receive at the *Bēma* for service in this life primarily deal with ruling with Christ in His kingdom. But desiring to rule with Christ is not like the struggle for power that we see in the world today. Christ's rule will be the greatest service that He can yet give the world. By His rule, He will serve the world with strength and compassion, and He will right all of the injustices of the present age.

God didn't keep rewards a secret; this is because He wants us to be motivated by them. They are one of many significant motivators He has given us.

Many have the mistaken idea that seeking rewards is selfish. But wanting to rule with Christ is not about a lust for power; it is about wanting greater opportunity to serve. In fact, if we want to have the best possible presentation at the Judgment Seat of Christ, we must labor in service in our own ministries and in support of other ministries, since those with whom we minister will be presented together with us at the *Bēma*.[19]

If we love Christ and His people, we will serve them now, and of course we will want every opportunity to serve them forever. Those whom He finds faithful in the very little tasks of service we have been given now will be rewarded with greater opportunities to serve forever in His kingdom. And there is nothing at all wrong with wanting our Lord and Savior Jesus Christ to be pleased with us and wanting to hear from Him, "Well done!"

Conclusion

Free Grace does teach us to turn from sins, and it is powerful to effect change. Even apart from the accountability of the Judgment Seat of Christ, Free Grace is able to produce godliness by removing all opportunity to boast in what Christ alone has done for us and by making us thankful for His inexpressible gift freely given, secure and steadfast. It also enables us to live by faith, rather than out of doubt and fear because God's "perfect love casts out fear" (1 John 4:18). All of this is what Paul means when he writes:

> For the grace of God has appeared, bringing salvation for all people, training us to renounce ungodliness and worldly passions, and to live self-controlled, upright, and godly lives in the present age, waiting for our blessed hope, the appearing of the glory of our great God and Savior Jesus Christ, who gave himself for us to redeem us from all lawlessness and to purify for himself a people for his own possession who are zealous for good works. (Titus 2:11-14)

In addition, accountability at the Judgment Seat of Christ teaches us to serve Christ and His Church. Turning from sins is not *optional*, and Free Grace theology does not teach that it is. We will be held accountable and there are consequences for how we live our lives, both for ourselves and others. If we sow edification to our brothers and sisters in Christ, we will reap rewards from the Lord, and they will be spurred on to greater service so that they too will reap greater rewards. If we sow bitterness and sin, we will reap loss of what might have been.

God uses grace, not fear, to teach us to live godly lives. Fear is as ineffective in producing godliness in us as nineteen years of hard labor was

---

[19] See Grant Hawley, "In This Life Together." Available online at http://boldgrace.org/articles/in-this-life-together.html. Last accessed, July, 29th, 2016.

ineffective in producing goodness in Jean Valjean. The gospel is magnified by counting Jesus Christ as the all-sufficient Savior He is and returning all of the glory of our salvation and its security to His worthy hands. The gospel is magnified in its effective power to produce godliness in God's children without intimidation and fear. And the gospel is magnified by letting grace be grace (relative to the free gift) and letting work be work (relative to the Judgment Seat of Christ). Thus, it is grace, free grace, that produces the transformation from within that God desires for us.

FULL ASSURANCE PRODUCES GODLY LIVING

By Charles C. Bing

I am a saved, born again Christian who will spend eternity with the Lord. "*Not so fast!*" some would say. "Have you examined your faith, your repentance, your commitment, and the amount of change in your life?" Others may even add, "Maybe we should wait to see how your life turns out before we make such a bold claim."

These objections raise some questions. Can Christians know for sure that they are saved, and if so, how? Does Free Grace theology give unsaved people a false assurance? Can doubts about one's salvation be healthy? Does having full assurance give people an excuse to sin or a motivation to godliness?

We will answer these questions by focusing on how Free Grace theology gives believers absolute assurance of salvation and how that assurance provides the *only* basis and the *best* motivation for godly living. The issue of assurance is important to many who are plagued with doubts about their salvation and struggle to move forward in living for God.

This Issue of Assurance

A discussion of how assurance of salvation relates to godly living must begin with a discussion of assurance itself. I believe that a person can have absolute assurance of salvation. Others teach that a person can have varying degrees of assurance and are vague about whether they think a person can have full assurance.[1] They teach that doubt about one's salvation is

---

[1] This chapter is primarily a response to Wayne Grudem, the most recent author to argue for this in *"Free Grace" Theology: 5 Ways It Diminishes the Gospel*. I have written a review of his book that addresses many other concerns outside the issue of assurance addressed in this chapter. It can be viewed at http://www.gracelife.org/resources/bookreviews. Other authors essentially promote the same view. See also John MacArthur, *The Gospel According to Jesus: What is Authentic Faith?*, revised and expanded anniversary ed. (Grand Rapids, MI: Zondervan, 2008);

a good motivation to godliness if that person is not living a godly life. While they would uphold the importance of God's Word, they do not believe it is sufficient proof for absolute assurance. They claim that assurance of salvation must also be based in a certain measure of fruitfulness or a changed life (with the evidence of good works) among other things.[2] In their view, a person who believes the gospel in God's Word (believes in Jesus Christ as Savior) but lives sinfully, can have a false assurance, not really be saved, and go to hell. They say that the Free Grace view of salvation by grace alone through faith alone gives unbelievers a dangerous false assurance.[3]

Does it magnify or diminish the gospel to tell people they can be sure of their salvation based on their faith in Christ as promised in His Word? Or does it magnify or diminish the gospel to tell people they may have assurance based on their faith in Christ as promised in His Word if it includes a certain level of personal performance such as turning from sin and a changed life? The reader must decide. Until we properly understand this issue of assurance, we cannot really discuss its impact on one's godliness.

What Do We Mean by Assurance?

By assurance of salvation, we mean the subjective acceptance of the fact that our salvation is secure in the present and the future. It is the conviction that we are indeed saved eternally. I am talking about an absolute or full assurance, not a reasonable, probable, partial, tentative, conditional, or probationary assurance. I find no logical or biblical category for partial assurance, which would be like insisting on an uncertain certainty. Of course, for those who believe that salvation can be lost, absolute assurance is impossible from the start. They can only speak of a practical or relative assurance based on whether they are presently living the kind of life that keeps them saved. (We will not talk about the various opinions about what that life looks like or what sins would lose one's salvation, because

---

Faith Works: The Gospel According to the Apostles (Dallas, TX; Word, 1993); *Hard to Believe: The High Cost and Infinite Value of Following Jesus* (Nashville, TN: Thomas Nelson, 2003); Mike McKinley, *Am I Really a Christian?* (Wheaton, IL: Crossway, 2011); and Alan P. Stanley, *Salvation Is More Complicated than You Think: A Study on the Teachings of Jesus* (Colorado Springs, CO: Authentic Publishing, 2007).

2   Grudem, *"Free Grace" Theology*, pp. 88-89. He lists five bases for assurance: a changed life, the internal testimony of the Holy Spirit, the leading of the Spirit, a deep inner sense of reliance on Jesus Christ for salvation rather than reliance on oneself, and continuing in the faith.

3   *Ibid.*, pp. 77-97; also MacArthur, *The Gospel According to Jesus*, pp. 108-109; Stanley, *Salvation Is More Complicated than You Think*, pp. 1-19.

there is no definitive standard.) Likewise, if someone believes that one is only truly saved by persevering in faith and good works until the end of life, then absolute assurance is impossible, because no one knows what his or her future holds.

I happen to believe assurance of salvation is this simple: Jesus said, "Truly, truly, I say to you, whoever hears my word and believes him who sent me has eternal life. He does not come into judgment, but has passed from death to life" (John 5:24). The Apostle Paul states unequivocally and without qualification, "Believe on the Lord Jesus, and you will be saved" (Acts 16:31a). That is the promise of God, a promise meant to be believed—period. However, some teach that a person can be somewhat sure or mostly sure, but not absolutely sure about his salvation.[4]

Why Do So Many Lack Assurance?

I observe in America and around the world that the lack of assurance of salvation is pandemic in Christianity. It is not hard to understand why when we survey the landscape of Christian teaching. We could mention many reasons people may doubt their salvation:

- They never accepted the gospel and its offer, and thus are unsaved.
- They don't know if they are among the elect.
- They fail to grow spiritually and so fail to comprehend spiritual truth.
- They are living in sin, which can bring a sense of condemning guilt.
- They believe they can lose their salvation.
- They are looking to their feelings.

But in this chapter, we will discuss some views that undermine assurance by changing the gospel itself.

In his book denouncing the Free Grace view of full assurance, Wayne Grudem argues that assurance depends on five things: 1) "a changed life," 2) "the internal testimony of the Holy Spirit," 3) "the leading of the Spirit," 4) "a deep inner sense of reliance on (also described as "a personal, heart-felt trust in") Jesus Christ for salvation rather than reliance on

---

[4] Grudem uses the terms "weak assurance" and "strong assurance" depending on the amount of one's works (*"Free Grace" Theology*, p. 92). MacArthur speaks of "a measure of assurance" (*The Gospel According to Jesus*, p. 272).

oneself," and 5) "continuing in the faith."[5] It is easy to understand why those under this kind of teaching might doubt that they are saved. What makes Grudem's list so harmful is that it changes the gospel of grace. To him, assurance of salvation depends on one's performance instead of simply believing the gospel. He does not include the objective testimony of God's Word in his list of assurances. Because his requirements are subjective in nature, an unsaved person could actually adopt a false assurance.

It is no wonder then that Grudem says assurance is "complex,"[6] while others with a similar view have written books titled *Salvation Is More Complicated than You Think* and *Hard to Believe*.[7] Yes, their view is *complex, complicated,* and *hard*—too complex for an introspective person to rejoice in a sure salvation, too complicated for children, indeed, too hard for any honest person wrestling with sin, temptation, and an internet history. This subtle legalism complicates assurance beyond the biblical condition of faith in Christ as Savior while stifling joy and confidence and producing guilt, doubt, and insecurity.[8]

To further illustrate how complex this faulty view of assurance is, let us consider the main criteria these authors claim must be added to faith in Jesus Christ: good works. They often reference Matt 7:15-23 and the phrase "You will recognize them by their fruits"[9] or James 2:14-26 and the phrase "faith by itself, if it does not have works, is dead."[10] Since I deal with these passages in other books, I will only make a few general comments.

First, the passage from Matthew 7 is talking about how to identify false prophets, not false Christians. In order to understand the test for a false prophet, we must understand what is meant by *fruit*. It can't be good works and outward conduct, because the wolves in this passage look and evidently behave like sheep, and what looks like good works is condemned in vv 21-23. A comparison with Matt 12:33-37 shows that *fruit*

---

[5] Grudem, *"Free Grace" Theology*, pp. 88-89, 105.

[6] *Ibid.*, p. 106.

[7] See n. 1 on page 55 for bibliographic information.

[8] By legalism, I mean any view that adds unbiblical conditions of personal merit or performance for acceptance with God. In relationship to the gospel, it is the attitude that someone can do something to earn, keep, or prove salvation.

[9] Grudem, *"Free Grace" Theology*, p. 89; MacArthur, *The Gospel According to Jesus*, pp. 169, 203, 213-15; Stanley seems to base his entire book (*Salvation Is More Complicated than You Think*) on his interpretation of Matt 7:15-23, which he refers to constantly.

[10] Grudem, *"Free Grace" Theology*, pp. 80, 132-36. MacArthur, *The Gospel According to Jesus*, pp. 169; 186, 250; Stanley, *Salvation Is More Complicated than You Think*, pp. 16, 26, 38, 41, 192, 207.

refers to the words of these false prophets, the same test that we see in Deut 13:1-3, 5 and 18:20-22.[11]

I think we should be very concerned that those who hold this faulty view of assurance misuse Jas 2:14-26 in the same way the Roman Catholics, Jehovah's Witnesses, and Mormons misuse it. Like those aberrant groups, these Evangelicals also say that you have to have good works to prove and thus be sure you are saved, but the soteriology of those groups is quite different (*at least assumed to be*) from Protestant evangelical soteriology.[12] As I have noted in other studies, James is not talking about eternal salvation but is writing to Christians about the usefulness of their faith. Faith that works by helping others spares Christians from temporal discipline and a merciless judgment at the Judgment Seat of Christ.[13]

One big problem with the view that good works are necessary for assurance is that we rarely see a discussion of what is a *good work*.[14] This leads us to think that this view is only concerned with appearances. Indeed, legalism can always produce a good appearance and upright conduct, but good conduct with unworthy motives is not really the good work that God desires. Furthermore, everyone does good works of some kind. Even a Satanist will cuddle and nurture her children, a Mormon will provide for his family, and an average Joe in America will pay his bills, provide for his family, and even go to church. Are these good works? We cannot know what people are doing twenty-four hours a day or know what sins they have *stopped* doing. We may not know that someone who curses now and then used to curse every other sentence.

So even if we could agree on what a good work is, we would then have to agree on how many are enough to give a person assurance. If a man who struggled daily with internet porn becomes a Christian and now slips

[11] See Charles C. Bing, *Grace, Salvation, and Discipleship: How to Understand Some Difficult Bible Passages* (NP: Grace Theology Press, 2015), pp. 68-70. The reader must forgive frequent references to my own works, but space limitations and the number of Bible passages discussed prohibit in-depth treatments here. I have discussed many of the passages referenced in this chapter in more detail elsewhere.

[12] *Catechism of the Catholic Church*, parags. 162, 1815; https://www.jw.org/en/bible-teachings/questions/what-is-salvation/, last accessed August 9, 2016; https://www.mormon.org/beliefs/jesus-christ, last accessed August 9, 2016.

[13] Bing, *Grace, Salvation, and Discipleship*, pp. 211-16; and *Lordship Salvation: A Biblical Evaluation and Response*, 2nd GraceLife edition (Xulon Press, 2014), pp. 30-38. For a brief discussion of the Judgment Seat of Christ as a judgment facing all and only Christians, see *Grace, Salvation, and Discipleship*, pp. 28-29.

[14] Stanley, in *Salvation Is More Complicated Than You Think*, has a brief discussion on pp. 24-27. He distinguishes "two kinds of works," "man-made works" and "God-produced works." The latter must accompany faith. However, he asserts that only God knows the motivations behind one's works, which should suggest that introspection about one's works is a futile endeavor.

only once a month, is that being fruitful? Will he have to conquer the problem completely to realize assurance? And what about the lusts in his mind that remain and haunt him? How can we quantify other sins like pride, covetousness, and anger?

Complex indeed! *Impossible* would be more accurate; assurance by performance dies by a thousand qualifications. It is impossible to have absolute assurance based on works. Even if we have a good definition for good works (such as *acts done in obedience to God in the power of the Holy Spirit for the glory of God*), how can we know for certain that we see this in ourselves or others? The Apostle Paul warned the Corinthian church not to judge his ministry and motives, for he did not even dare to judge them himself, but he submitted himself to God's judgment (1 Cor 4:3-5a). If the Corinthians and Paul could not make an accurate assessment of his works and motives, it is obvious that we cannot judge works that prove our or others' salvation, especially in the absence of any objective defining criteria.

Many people have no assurance of salvation because they are trying to judge themselves, their faith, their repentance, or their works—a subjective and impossible endeavor.

Is Full Assurance Possible?

Most Christians would say that some level of assurance of salvation is possible. But when I refer to assurance, I mean *absolute and full* assurance of salvation beyond any doubt. I disagree with the view that assurance of salvation can be on a scale from weak to strong based on whether the person has "weak evidence of belief" or "strong evidence of belief."[15] Without a discernable baseline, we cannot know what comprises "weak evidence" or "strong evidence." *Miriam-Webster's Collegiate Dictionary* defines *assurance* using words like "pledge, guarantee, security, being certain in the mind"[16] and the online Miriam-Webster dictionary's relevant definitions are "the state of being sure or certain about something" and "a strong feeling of confidence about yourself or about being right."[17] The *American Heritage Dictionary* defines *assurance* as "Freedom from doubt;

---

[15] Grudem, *"Free Grace" Theology*, p. 92.

[16] *Miriam-Webster's Collegiate Dictionary*, 11th ed. "assurance."

[17] Miriam-Webster online dictionary, "assurance." http://www.merriam-webster.com/dictionary/assurance. Last accessed, September 21st, 2016.

certainty about something."[18] These dictionary definitions leave no room for degrees of doubt.

God's Word Teaches Full Assurance

Our view of assurance shouldn't be determined by a dictionary definition; God's Word is the final measure. When the Apostle Paul declares to the Ephesian church, "For by grace you have been saved through faith. And this is not your own doing; it is the gift of God" (Eph 2:8), he cites no ancillary conditions for this statement of certainty. He also says in Eph 2:10 that Christians are "created in Christ Jesus for good works, which God prepared beforehand that we should walk in them," which means that good works are God's purpose and desire for us *after* we are saved. It is in no way a statement of another condition, a guaranteed result, or a proof for salvation.[19] The fact that God promises salvation in Christ and I accept that promise as true and believe in Christ is enough to give me full assurance.

But, Grudem objects, the question is not whether we believe in the Word of God as the sufficient basis of assurance. He says, "the truthfulness of Scripture does not answer the other aspect of assurance, the question, 'How can I know that I personally have believed these things?'"[20] To this we would simply reply that *the Scripture does not ask such a question, nor should we!* It is a fabricated construct necessitated by a theological system that requires works to prove one's faith. The question does not make sense. I know when I believe something. I know that I believe God's Word and I know that I believe in Jesus Christ as my Savior for eternal salvation.

Full assurance comes from keeping our focus on Christ. The moment we turn inward, we can have doubts. We do not ask a man on a ladder if he *personally believes* the ladder will support him. He believes it will, and he knows that he believes. To question whether he *personally believes* just muddies the water. How else does one believe something? To be saved, a person must believe the person of Christ, the provision of Christ, and also the promise of Christ. That promise does have a personal element to it, because it is promised to every person. To be saved, I must believe

---

[18]   *The American Heritage Dictionary of the English Language*, https://www.ahdictionary.com/word/search.html?q=assurance&submit.x=50&submit.y=25. Last Accessed, September 21st, 2016.

[19]   See Bing, *Grace, Salvation, and Discipleship*, pp. 176-77; *Lordship Salvation*, pp. 45-46.

[20]   Grudem, *"Free Grace" Theology*, p. 94. He also says we should ask, "How do I know that I have truly believed?" (p. 85).

that the promise of eternal life is for me *specifically*. That is different from using the redundancy *personally believes* to make a distinction from one who simply believes.

When speaking of salvation, the New Testament simply does not use qualifiers with *believe* and *faith* like *personally* believe, *truly* believe, *really* believe, *sincerely* believe, *heartfelt* belief, or *genuine* faith. Nor does it use negative disqualifiers like *spurious* faith, *false* faith, *insincere* faith, *head* faith, or *superficial* faith. Why? Because it is not technically faith or the kind of faith that saves us; it is the *object* of faith that saves us. Faith is the instrumental means by which God's grace is communicated to us in His saving person, the Lord Jesus Christ. The emphasis in the Bible is on the veracity of the object of faith, Jesus Christ. If we deem Him trustworthy, then we believe in Him for eternal salvation. Think about this: a Buddhist believes in Buddha for salvation, a Muslim believes in Allah and his prophet Muhammad for salvation, a Christian believes in Jesus Christ for salvation. Who is saved? The Christian of course, because he has believed in Jesus Christ as the One who is most trustworthy. He is not saved by how he believes, how sincerely he believes, or how much belief he has. Belief is belief. It is the object of one's belief that makes the eternal difference.

I realize many theologians and commentators like to put saving faith in a special theological category, but the faith I have in Jesus Christ is the same as the faith I have that $1 + 1 = 2$. I do not have a *heartfelt* faith in this mathematical truth; I am simply convinced that it is true so that I trust it when needed. It goes beyond Scripture to psychologize faith into three elements—knowledge, assent, and trust.[21] This can easily undermine assurance (Did I believe with my head and not my heart and my will?). Yet the New Testament does not dissect faith in this way or raise that question. In fact, in the New Testament both the *mind* and *heart* are used to refer to the inner person and the moral attitude.[22] One can find appeals to salvation that appear to address a particular aspect of the inner person, but that could be for the sake of emphasis depending on the person's disposition.[23] I have heard testimonies from good Christian friends

---

[21] *Ibid.*, pp. 72-73. In this definition of faith, trust refers to the will. However, this model of faith relies on a tautology, because faith is defined by *fiducia*, which is Latin for *faith*. See my discussion in Bing, *Lordship Salvation*, p. 59.

[22] E.g., Matt 9:4; Rom 1:21, 28; 7:23, 25; 2 Cor 4:6; Eph 4:17, 23; Phil 4:7; Col 2:18; Heb 8:10.

[23] Sometimes Scripture appears to emphasize the intellect and understanding (e.g., Matt 11:25-27; John 6:69; 20:31 Acts 26:28), but other times the will (e.g., Matt 23:37; John 5:40; Acts 13:46; 16:31; 17:30; 1 John 3:23).

who have been saved through each of these emphases. It would be more biblical to say that faith involves the inner person and not go beyond that.

Absolute assurance is possible only by looking beyond ourselves to the Savior. *Faith is not our Savior; Jesus Christ is our Savior.*

God's Promises Assume Assurance

The demand that we inspect our works or our faith implies it is presumptuous to know for certain that we are saved based on the Word of God alone. But I think it is presumptuous to question God's promise of eternal life to all who believe in Jesus Christ. Are we deceiving ourselves to claim we are absolutely sure we are saved based on what God has provided in Jesus Christ? I think we are in danger of self-deception when we put our subjective judgment of our performance over God's objective judgment of Christ's performance. Scripture shows that we can assume without doubt that those who believe in Christ for eternal salvation are saved eternally.[24] God does not lie (Rom 3:4; Titus 1:2); His Word is sufficient for absolute assurance of salvation; therefore, when we read in Scripture that salvation is contingent upon belief in Christ, we know that a believer's eternal salvation is assumed and he can be sure of it.

The Believer's Faith Assumes Assurance

It is not foolish to claim that you know you have believed in Christ as Savior. It would be more foolish to claim that you do *not* know whether you have believed in Christ as Savior. *Who else would know?* Faith is the assurance that something is true (Heb 11:1). That is why Scripture does not ask how you can know whether you have *personally* believed in Christ. Reformed Calvinist scholar Michael Eaton observes how modern Reformed theology has drifted from the view that faith is assurance:

> "The Reformation tradition has always made much of assurance of salvation. For Luther and Calvin faith is assurance. Subsequent theological reflection drove a wedge between initial-faith which may or may not include full assurance of

---

[24] E.g., John 1:12; 3:16, 36; 5:24; 6:40, 47; 11:25-27; 20:31; Acts 13:48; 16:31; Rom 3:22-24; 4:23-25; 5:1-2; Gal 2:16; 3:24-26; Eph 1:13-14; 2:8-9.

salvation, and developed-faith which reflects upon itself and reaches assurance of salvation."[25]

Faith in something indicates certainty and conviction that the object of faith is trustworthy. The nature of faith as assurance will be discussed later.

New Testament Writers Assumed Assurance

It is possible that the Gospels' authors, especially John, wrote their Gospels with unbelievers in mind, although most of Matthew, Mark, and Luke is discipleship truth for believers (as differentiated from salvation truth for unbelievers).[26] The book of Revelation, though certainly written to encourage Christians, also contains warnings and invitations to unbelievers.

But in the Epistles, it is clear that the authors are writing to believers and churches to either rebuke their ungodliness or encourage their godliness. They may write *about* unbelievers, but their words are to believers. Consider this:

- No author questions his readers' salvation.
- No author invites his readers to believe in Christ as Savior.
- The authors use exhortations that apply to Christians.
- The authors consider even sinning Christians as true believers.
- The authors do not signal changes to address a different group of readers that are not Christians.
- The authors use the readers' assurance of salvation as a motivation to live a godly life.

I realize that some will cite passages they think disprove my assertions about the Epistles. Some examples that explain what those passages mean will be discussed later.

---

[25] Michael A. Eaton, *No Condemnation: A Theology of Assurance of Salvation* (Downers Grove, IL: InterVarsity Press, 1997), p. 27.

[26] I am fully aware that those who are Reformed or Arminian usually conflate salvation and discipleship. They believe every Christian is a disciple, because they interpret the conditions for discipleship in the Gospels as conditions for salvation. This premise is reflected in their performance-based view of assurance and confuses justification and sanctification. See my discussions in *Grace, Salvation, and Discipleship*, pp. 52-54 and in *Lordship Salvation*, pp. 129-74.

New Testament Exhortations Require Assurance

The many exhortations of the Epistles' authors only make sense if the readers know they are Christians. It would be putting the theological cart before the horse (sanctification truth before justification truth) to exhort unbelievers to obey and live godly lives. It would be both confusing and frustrating to unsaved readers to have to fulfill a moral code in order to be considered true believers. Unsaved readers would lack the motivation and the power of the Holy Spirit to fulfill these commands on any level more than the flesh.

On the contrary, what we see in the Epistles is the assumption of the readers' salvation as a basis for the authors' ethical appeals (e.g., Rom 12:1; Eph 4:1; Col 2:6). In the controversial passages in Hebrews and James, the authors also refer to their readers as believers. In the Epistles, the writers appeal to the readers to live up to what they know they are, not obey commands to prove or discover that they are saved.

What Makes Full Assurance Possible?

Full assurance of salvation comes from a biblical understanding of grace's role in salvation and the Christian life, a healthy view of the sufficiency of Scripture, a proper understanding of faith as assurance, and a proper perspective about other evidences of salvation.

The Provision of Unconditional Grace

Free grace is another way of describing unconditional, undeserved, unmerited grace. If one misunderstands or ignores God's grace in salvation, there will be a skewed view of assurance of salvation. Without the unconditional grace of God, we are left to examine our faith and our performance.[27]

---

[27] Wayne Grudem criticizes Free Grace theology and the Free Grace Alliance view of assurance, but does not define or discuss grace in his book. He calls his view the "non-Free Grace" view (*"Free Grace" Theology*, p. 25). His General Index has numerous listings for *faith* and *repentance*, but there is not one listing for *grace*. In frequent appeals to the Reformers, Grudem refers to their credo of *sola fide*, but never their credo of *sola gratia*. This de-emphasis of grace reveals the root of his errant soteriology and its result—an elusive assurance. In contrast, the essential role and nature of grace is exemplified in the Free Grace Alliance Covenant which begins, "The Grace of God in justification is an unconditional free gift." From this comes their view that "Assurance of justification is the birthright of every believer from the moment of faith in Jesus Christ…" (See "Mission & Beliefs," http://www.freegracealliance.com/about-us/covenant. Last accessed September 24th, 2016).

The book of Romans develops the theology of the gospel of grace and its assurance more than any other book of the Bible. There the Apostle Paul emphasizes the freeness of God's grace by using a literary redundancy in Rom 3:24: "freely by His grace."[28] He also uses Abraham as an example of someone saved by faith in God's provision and promise (Rom 4:1-3) who was sure of God's blessing and salvation, because his faith rested on unconditional grace: "That is why it depends on faith, in order that the promise may rest on grace and be guaranteed to all his offspring…" (Rom 4:16a). The assurance of blessing comes from grace through faith. Abraham's faith is not qualified or described; rather, the emphasis is on the object of his faith, because that is what gives assurance. Whether Abraham had a sincere or heartfelt faith is not in the purview of this Scripture (or any other, for that matter).

We do not have space to discuss all of the assurances of grace that the Apostle Paul emphasizes in Romans (for some other examples, see Rom 4:4-5; 5:20; 8:28-39; 11:26, 29).

But we should note that Paul ends his theological discussion of grace with a doxology (Rom 11:33-36). Grace always reserves praise and glory for God. No one can boast or glory in his own works as necessary for or proof of his salvation (cf. Gal 6:14; Eph 2:8-9). The gospel of the Reformers, *sola gratia* and *sola fide*, allowed them to also proclaim *soli Deo gloria* (to God alone be the glory).

Unconditional grace gives us assurance of salvation while giving God the glory, and therefore it magnifies His gospel. This is quite different from saying that works or a certain kind of faith give us assurance of salvation. The latter view diminishes the glory due to God because it diminishes the authority of His gospel and His Word.

The Objective Testimony of God's Word

God's Word is an unchanging standard in contrast to our feelings, works, or opinions about our faith. There is no way to give anyone absolute assurance of salvation by appealing to variable self-evaluations about how much or what kind of faith one has in Jesus Christ as Savior.

To believe God's Word is to believe God Himself. It is not so much a matter of *what* one believes as it is *whom* one believes. God's promise comes through Scripture, not some other revelation or inward feeling.

---

[28] The word *dōrean* describes how we are justified by grace (*chariti*) and means to be "freely given, as a gift, without payment, gratis." BDAG, s.v. "*dōrean*."

Scripture has to be sufficient because it is *God's* Word. The Reformers understood this when they chose to side with God's Word over the Catholic church and the traditions of men. Along with *sola gratia, sola fide,* and *soli Deo Gloria,* they proclaimed *sola Scriptura* (Scripture alone). Their adherence to Scripture is seen in the Belgic Confession (1561), considered one of the best official statements of the Reformed faith:

> We believe that those Holy Scriptures fully contain the will of God, and that whatsoever man ought to believe, unto salvation, is sufficiently taught therein...For, since it is forbidden, to add unto or take away anything from the word of God, it does thereby evidently appear, that the doctrine thereof is most perfect and complete in all respects. *Neither may we consider any writing of men, however holy these men may have been, of equal value with those divine Scriptures, nor ought we to consider custom, or the great multitude, or antiquity, or succession of times and persons, or councils, decrees or statutes, as of equal value with the truth of God, for the truth is above all...*[29]

It is disappointing today to see, in contradiction to this confession, how frequently Reformed Calvinists argue for conditional assurance by citing creeds and traditional interpretations. This diminishes the authority of Scripture, which is perhaps why we find so little interaction on the Bible texts themselves when these authors criticize the Free Grace view of assurance or other Free Grace views.[30] In general, I notice a much greater tendency for Free Grace proponents to emphasize the Bible in context than do Reformed Calvinists.[31]

When allowed to speak for itself in context, the Bible shows that a person who believes in Christ can know with absolute certainty that he is saved. As Bible expositor H. A. Ironside said, "It is the blood of Christ

---

[29] *Belgic Confession,* First Electronic Edition, (n.p.: Fig Books, 2012), Article VII. Emphasis added.

[30] For example, Grudem's first argument against Free Grace theology is an appeal to the Reformers and creeds (*"Free Grace" Theology,* pp. 27-39), but references to these as well as contemporary theologians are found throughout the book to dismiss Free Grace interpretations. He uses Scriptures also, but more as proof texts and generally without detailed contextual discussions.

[31] One example of this is how Grudem criticizes my view of repentance in my book, *Lordship Salvation.* There I argue for the change of mind view in a three-page discussion of dictionary entries (Bing, *Lordship Salvation,* pp. 67-69), which Grudem criticizes using *ten pages* in his book (*"Free Grace" Theology,* pp. 54-64; he does not understand my main point that *repentance* meant a *change of mind* in New Testament times, but is then interpreted theologically and incorrectly in the Bible as *sorrow for sins* or *turning from sins*). He then dismisses my eighteen-page, in-depth, contextual discussions of specific Bible passages on repentance (Bing, *Lordship Salvation,* pp. 70-88) in *one sentence* (Grudem, *"Free Grace" Theology,* p. 64).

that makes us safe and the Word of God that makes us sure."[32] What the Bible does not reveal is any such question as "How can I know that I personally have believed these things?" Are we to believe the Bible or a theologically contrived question?

The Nature of Faith as Assurance

The question "How can I know that I personally have believed these things?" is pointless because faith by its very nature includes assurance (Heb 11:1).[33] We believe something because we are sure about it; we consider it true and trustworthy. Our belief may be misplaced, but it is sure, even if it is surely wrong. We can believe that 1 + 1 = 3 even though it is not true. Our faith is not in question, but its object. When someone believes in Jesus Christ, that person is expressing certainty that who He is, what He provides, and what He promises are true and trustworthy. Assurance of salvation comes from the objective fact that God's Word is true about these things, and that the person knows and believes them. On the basis of biblical revelation, we can *know* that we have eternal life (1 John 5:13) in the same way we can know that Jesus is God or that God loves us.

It is futile and unbiblical to question *what kind of faith* is required for salvation. There may be little faith or great faith, but there is only one kind of faith—the certain conviction that something is true and trustworthy. Since that is what faith means, having doubt and belief about something is mutually exclusive and logically impossible.

The Role of Subjective Evidence

Some believe that assurance of salvation is like a three-legged stool; it depends on the testimony of Scripture, the presence of good works, and the inner testimony of the Holy Spirit. Contrary to this notion, I have argued for the sufficiency of the Scripture alone to give us full assurance.

The evidence of one's good works cannot provide absolute assurance because there are no defining standards of measurement. At best, one's works can provide supporting evidence, but not final proof. As I noted

---

[32] H. A. Ironside, *Full Assurance: How to Know You're Saved* (Chicago, IL: Moody Press, 1968), p. 29.

[33] The general idea of assurance in the New Testament is sometimes conveyed by the words used for *faith, pistis* (Acts 17:31, translated "assurance" in NKJV and ESV, "proof" in NASB, NIV, and NET), and *believe, pisteuō* (2 Tim 3:14; "been assured of" in NKJV, "become convinced of" in NASB, NIV, "confident about" in NET, "have firmly believed" in ESV).

earlier, in discussions about the necessity of works to prove the genuine-
ness of one's faith, there is rarely, if ever, a definition of what a good work
is. Until we have that, how can we measure anything? When we try to
specify what comprises a good work, we run into the problems already
mentioned. Good works can be mimicked, imitated, manufactured from
bad motives, a response to legalism, subjective, relative, or unseen, and
therefore unreliable as proof of salvation. The best we can say is that they
offer evidence of salvation.

So it is legitimate to ask,

- "How can we discern what is a genuine good work?"
- "How many good works does a person need to demonstrate to
  be sure of salvation?"
- "How long does a person have to demonstrate those works?"
- "How much does a person's life have to change?"

I think 2 Cor 5:17 is regretfully misused to argue that a person's conduct must show a total change: "Therefore, if anyone is in Christ, he is a
new creation. The old has passed away; behold the new has come." In the
context, the passage is not speaking of conduct, but the way a person sees
Jesus Christ and the world in a new way (cf. 2 Cor 5:16).[34] Obviously,
anyone who is born again does become a new creation, and, I believe,
will have a changed life with some fruit or good works. But having said
that, I can't prove it from Scripture or by what I observe in that person. In
the Bible, fruit resulting from salvation is exhorted, implied by precept,
and demonstrated by example, but no statement makes fruit required or
guaranteed, much less quantifiable. If good works are guaranteed, then
why do we have all of the New Testament exhortations to do good works?

Neither can the inner testimony of the Holy Spirit be used as proof of
salvation, if that is how one interprets Rom 8:16: "The Spirit himself bears
witness with our spirit that we are children of God." This also is too subjective. Since feelings and perceptions change, the Holy Spirit's inner testimony is vulnerable to our subjective judgment. At most, we can view the
Holy Spirit's inner testimony as another evidence of salvation, not a proof.

Introspection is subjective by definition. Examination of our works,
motives, feelings, or the testimony of the Holy Spirit can yield corrobo-
rating evidence of salvation—*or not*; results will vary. The biblical promise

---

[34] For a more detailed explanation, see Bing, "GraceNotes – no. 64," available online at http://www.
gracelife.org/resources/gracenotes/?id=64. Last accessed, September 24th, 2016.

of God's grace appropriated through faith in Jesus Christ is the rock-solid, objective measure of our assurance of salvation.

Are Doubts about Salvation Good?

Many who are truly saved doubt their salvation (just as many who are not saved doubt theirs). Before we discuss the issue of doubts, we should agree that *no one ever has been or will be saved by anything other than God's free grace through faith alone in Jesus Christ alone.*[35] However, after salvation Christians can soon become confused by the various deviations from that truth within evangelical Christianity. If they become confused about the gospel, or the freeness of God's grace, or the simple condition of believing in the gospel, then they may have doubts about their salvation. Those doubts are good only if they drive someone to clarify the truth so that they find assurance.

If a person understands the gospel so that he has believed in Jesus Christ and received eternal life, what profit is there in introducing doubts about his salvation on the basis of his struggle with sin and sanctification issues? Do we tell him to look within to see if he truly believed with his heart and embraced Jesus Christ in a personal relationship, or ask if he has turned from all his sins, or surrendered and submitted all of his life to Him as Master? These introspective and subjective conditions will only confuse an individual. Jesus and the New Testament authors do not challenge the salvation of their audiences with such questions.

The main text used to promote self-examination for proof of salvation is 2 Cor 13:5,[36] "Examine yourselves, to see whether you are in the faith. Test yourselves. Or do you not realize this about yourselves, that Jesus Christ is in you?—unless indeed you fail to meet the test!" The usual interpretation assumes that Paul is telling the Corinthian readers to look within themselves to see if they are truly saved—"Is Jesus Christ really in you?" But the context shows that it is not Paul's intent to question their salvation; he is actually *affirming* their salvation. I and others have

---

[35] Even though he opposes Free Grace theology, I believe Wayne Grudem was saved by a gospel of free grace, because there is no other way. So it is contradictory when he insists "good works are a necessary *result* of saving faith" (Grudem, *"Free Grace" Theology*, p. 39; emphasis added), because this actually concedes that at the moment someone is saved, faith is alone and unaccompanied by works, since works are a result.

[36] E.g., Grudem, *"Free Grace" Theology*, pp. 80-81, 130-31; MacArthur, *The Gospel According to Jesus*, pp. 39, 213, 220.

written about this passage in detail elsewhere,[37] so here is a simple summary from the context. First, Paul knows he is writing to believers (cf. 2 Cor 1:21-22; 3:2-3; 6:14; 8:9; 13:11-14). Second, in the Corinthian Epistles, he is defending the authenticity of his apostleship (2 Cor 5:12-13; 10:1–11:33; 12:11-33). Here he defends his credibility with a simple argument using irony—I paraphrase: "You are questioning my credibility as an apostle, but you don't need to examine *me*; examine *yourselves*. Is Jesus Christ in you? Of course He is! And since you heard about Christ from me, that proves my authenticity!" The Corinthian believers are his credentials of authenticity (cf. 2 Cor 3:1-3).

The other go-to text used to promote self-examination is First John. The commentary tradition treats this epistle as John's tests of salvation. Indeed, John gives his readers many tests, but are the tests designed to prove their *salvation*, or their *fellowship* with God?[38] John clearly believes his readers are saved (cf. 1 John 2:1, 12-14, 18, 20, 27; 3:1-2; 5:13-14), which is why he states his purpose in the introduction as a desire for them to have fellowship with the apostles and with Jesus Christ (1:3-4). Again, I have written on how we should understand this epistle and these tests, so I will not repeat myself here.[39] It would be impossible for any Christian to have full assurance of salvation based on these tests.[40]

If someone is not saved, doubts about his relationship to God may motivate that person to seek the answers that will save him. However, if one has believed in Jesus Christ as directed by Scripture, interjecting doubts about that one's salvation cannot be healthy. The simple relationship of parent and child is an example. The basis for growth, maturity, and

---

[37] See Bing, *Grace, Salvation, and Discipleship*, pp. 168-70; also Bing, "GraceNotes – no.53," available online at http://www.gracelife.org/resources/gracenotes/?id=53; and Perry C. Brown, "What Is the Meaning of 'Examine Yourselves' in 2 Corinthians 13:5?" *Bibliotheca Sacra* 154 (April-June 1997): 175-88. For a slightly different Free Grace interpretation, see Andy Woods, "Doesn't Second Corinthians 13:5 Say We Need to Examine Ourselves to See if We Are Saved?" in *21 Tough Questions about Grace*, Hawley, ed., pp. 215-25.

[38] The word for *fellowship, koinōnia*, means "close association involving mutual interests and sharing, *association, communion, fellowship, close relationship*." BDAG, s.v. "*koinōnia*." It is not a synonym for salvation, but salvation is the basis for fellowship.

[39] Charles C. Bing, "Does First John Tell Us How to Know We Are Saved" in *21 Tough Questions about Grace*, pp. 203-213; and *Grace, Salvation, and Discipleship*, pp. 228-38.

[40] Ironically, a number of authors use First John to try to give assurance of salvation. One of the earlier commentators, Robert Law (*The Tests of Life: A Study of the First Epistles of St. John* [Edinburgh: T. & T. Clark, 1909]) lists three tests; John MacArthur (*Saved without a Doubt: How to Be Sure of Your Salvation* [Wheaton, IL: Victor Books, 1992]) has eleven tests; Steven J. Lawson (*Absolutely Sure* [Sisters, OR: Multnomah Publishers, 1999]) finds nine, and Mike McKinley (*Am I Really a Christian?* [Wheaton, IL: Crossway, 2011]) has five. See also Christopher D. Bass, *That You May Know: Assurance of Salvation in 1 John* (Nashville, TN: B & H Publishing Group, 2008).

deepening intimacy in that relationship is primarily the unconditional love and acceptance of the parent. The child lives confidently, knowing that he or she has the freedom to fail but never forfeit or be denied that relationship. But if that child is treated with conditional love and tentative acceptance based on his performance while growing up, it is hard to imagine a healthy and secure relationship with his parents later. Doubt about another's love and acceptance does not promote intimate fellowship.

By divine design, God has chosen to relate to His children as Father. God has given us a paradigm by which we can know and experience His unconditional love and grace. He wants us to live our new lives in His family with the confidence of full acceptance, that is, the full assurance of salvation. God knows that *we cannot grow forward if we keep looking backward*, wondering if we are saved or if He accepts us.

Full Assurance as the Basis for Godly Living

Many Christians may not think much about why they do what they do for God. Motivations are sometimes hard to judge, but they are very important for a godly life. Legalism, guilt, and doubt can never motivate someone to the godliness that God desires.

The Best Motivations for Godly Living

When we discuss godly living, motives are crucial. Why be good or godly? We should agree that the highest motivations are love and gratitude. In 1 John 4:19 we read, "We love because he first loved us" and in Rom 12:1 we are urged to give ourselves to God as living sacrifices "by the mercies of God," the grace that the Apostle Paul explained in Romans chapters 1-11. The more I understand God's unremitting love and unconditional grace, the more I want my life to be a thank You note to God. I want to reciprocate His love and therefore obey Him.

Whenever we teach the abundance of God's grace in a passage like Rom 5:20 ("Now the law came in to increase the trespass, but where sin increased, grace abounded all the more"), someone will object that such free and super-abundant grace will lead Christians to license. Paul anticipated this objection and answers it twice in Romans chapter 6 by saying "By no means!" (vv 2, 15), as he argues that Christians have a new identity (vv 3-8), a new power (vv 9-14), a new Master (vv 15-19), and a new accountability with consequences (vv 20-23).

The argument that grace breeds license is a straw man that usually comes from a fabricated hypothetical scenario. Surely, there *are* Christians who use grace as an excuse to live licentiously, but I have never met anyone who has demonstrated that or argued that way to me. On the other hand, I have met thousands of Christians who, because of their love and gratitude for God's grace in Christ, choose to live for Christ and share His message, sometimes at great personal sacrifice.

Fear bred by doubt about future consequences is a motivation found in the Bible, but it is not intended to undermine the believer's assurance of salvation. Fear and doubt can be used to keep Christians from turning away from Christ (e.g., the warnings in Hebrews and Galatians), from continuing in sin (e.g., 1 Cor 11:28-30; 2 Cor 13:1-2; 2 Thess 3:6-15; Jas 2:1-13; 5:19-20), or to remind them to live responsibly in view of the future Judgment Seat of Christ where every Christian will have to give an account for his or her life (2 Cor 5:10). There is much more that should be said about the Judgment Seat of Christ because it is too seldom taught, even though it gives Christians another motivation to live a godly life. It accomplishes this not by threatening the loss of salvation or undermining assurance of salvation, but through the promises and warnings about rewards enjoyed or denied in eternity.

The Biblical Appeals for Godliness Based on the Assumption of Salvation

In the New Testament, appeals for godliness assume the salvation of the reader.[41] No author would appeal to an unbeliever to live a godly life apart from having a regenerated life.

While the four Gospels' authors certainly had readers who were both believers and unbelievers, we never find Jesus questioning the salvation of those the authors state have believed in Him. Appeals to godliness and the commitments of discipleship are directed to those who are saved or prospects for salvation. In John 8:30-31, John records that many Jews believed in Christ, yet Christ says to those who believed, "If you abide in my word, you are truly my disciples." Here is an appeal for a commitment to continue[42] in His Word as disciples based on the fact that they had just

---

[41] However, in the Gospels some of Jesus' appeals for godliness were made to the unbelieving nation of Israel to indict them for not keeping the Mosaic Law, or to hypocrites to expose their self-righteousness (e.g., Matt 6:1-4, 16-18; 7:1-6; 19:16-22).

[42] The word *abide* (from *menō*) does not mean *believe*, but *to adhere to, continue in, remain in.* BDAG, s.v. "*menō*."

believed in Him. In John, we also see the upper room discourse in chapters 13–17, which is sanctification truth based on the fact that Jesus knew the eleven disciples were saved.

Likewise, the writers of the New Testament epistles do not question the salvation of their readers, but assume it in their exhortations for godliness. Appeals for godly living are often made on the basis of and the reminder of the fact that the readers were indeed saved. We have already discussed the progression of Romans. Here are some other examples that show that the authors of the epistles exhorted the readers based on the assumption of their new identity and position in Christ:

The Corinthians

Here is a church with a lot of problems, or we could say, here are a lot of people behaving sinfully. Yet in his opening words, the Apostle Paul reminds them of their saved status as "those sanctified in Christ Jesus" (1 Cor 1:2). Even the carnal church members are called "infants in Christ" (1 Cor 3:1). After listing and warning them about sinful behaviors that characterize unbelievers, Paul appeals to them as those washed, sanctified, and justified in Jesus Christ (1 Cor 6:9-11). Even those believers who sinned at the Lord's Supper, got sick, and died were considered disciplined by the Lord, not unsaved (1 Cor 11:30-32). His farewell words in Second Corinthians call them "brothers" and exhort them as such (2 Cor 13:11-14).

The Galatians

This group also had serious problems. They were beginning to turn from the gospel of grace back to the Law, yet Paul depicts their conduct as deserting Christ who called them (Gal 1:6). Again, they are addressed as Christian "brothers" from the beginning of his letter to the end (Gal 1:11; 4:12, 28; 6:1, 18). They had believed in Christ and received His Spirit (Gal 3:2-3). His final exhortations are to stand firm in the gospel of grace that saved them, not to *really* believe in Christ as Savior (Gal 5:1ff).

The Ephesians

Paul reminds the readers in Ephesus of their salvation and its blessings in chapters 1–3, he then begins practical exhortations in Eph 4:1 by appealing to them "to walk in a manner worthy of the calling to which you have been called…"

The Colossians

Paul follows the familiar pattern of beginning his letter by reminding the readers of their status in Christ (Col 1:2). He thanks God for their faith and love that are the fruit of the gospel they believed (Col 1:3-7). Since they have "received Christ Jesus the Lord," Paul exhorts them to "walk in him" (Col 2:6). There is no doubt that they are believers, so when we come to the conditional statement in Col 1:23, we see that Paul is not making their *salvation* conditioned on their continuation in "the faith" (a reference to Christian truth and its privileges, not subjective faith).[43] Because they have been reconciled to God (Col 1:22), the condition of faithful perseverance is to obtain a favorable presentation to Christ at the Judgment Seat of Christ, an accounting for believers only.[44]

The Hebrews

In spite of their movement away from Christianity to Judaism, the author of this epistle constantly refers to his readers in Christian terms, even in the warning passages. There are no structural or grammatical indications that he changes from addressing believers to unbelievers. In fact, some of the author's strongest affirmations of their saved status come alongside the strongest threats of divine discipline in the warning passages. There are many such observations that can be made here, and I have done so elsewhere.[45]

Peter's Readers

Peter begins his first epistle with a reminder that his readers have been "born again" (1 Pet 1:3) and his second epistle with a reminder that they "have obtained a faith of equal standing with ours by the righteousness of our God and Savior Jesus Christ" (2 Pet 1:1). That is why 2 Pet 1:10

---

[43] He does not say "in your faith," but "in the faith" (*tē pistei*).

[44] See Bing, *Grace, Salvation, and Discipleship*, pp. 184-86; see also my article "The Warning in Colossians 1:21-23," *Bibliotheca Sacra* 164 (January-March 2007): 74-88.

[45] Bing, *Grace, Salvation, and Discipleship*, pp. 195-208, and my article "Does Fire in Hebrews Refer to Hell?" *Bibliotheca Sacra* 167 (July-September 2010): 342-57.

(often used to argue for introspection)[46] should not be viewed as an exhortation for the readers to prove their salvation to themselves, but an exhortation to demonstrate their salvation to others.[47] Even in his discussion of unsaved false prophets (2 Pet 2:1-17), we note that Peter refers to them in the third person as he also does some who were apparently saved and in the church but influenced by their false teaching (2 Pet 2:18-22).[48] His final exhortation to the readers is to "grow in the grace and knowledge of our Lord and Savior Jesus Christ" (2 Pet 3:18a).

These are just some of the many examples of exhortations to godliness based on an assumption of the readers' salvation. We do not see evangelistic invitations given to any of the readers, though many of them have erred morally or theologically.

The Godly Results of Full Assurance

I have argued that full assurance produces God-pleasing results. I will now develop that thought further with more reasons and some personal insights.

In Our Disposition in Life

From my observation and the testimonies of many people who understand salvation from a Free Grace perspective, I see a common experience of freedom that brings joy to the soul. I have collected and saved hundreds of testimonies to that effect from pastors and people around the world. I do not see or hear about that joy in churches that undermine assurance of salvation.

My wife befriended a Christian woman we will call Nicki. She told my wife that when she believed in Jesus Christ as Savior she was overjoyed, "floating on clouds" in her words. About six months after her salvation, she went to her church where she exhibited this bubbly joy. An undoubtedly well-intentioned older lady cautioned her, "Be careful, because if you sin you will lose your salvation." Nicki said her joy and peace immediately

---

[46] E.g., Grudem, *"Free Grace" Theology*, pp. 85-86, 95; Stanley, *Salvation Is More Complicated than You Think*, p. 3.

[47] The goal of his exhortation is not the *fact* of the readers' entrance into God's kingdom, but the *quality* of that entrance, described in v 11 by "there will be richly provided for you an entrance." For a more detailed discussion of this passage, see *Grace, Salvation, and Discipleship*, pp. 222-24.

[48] See my discussion in *Grace, Salvation, and Discipleship*, pp. 224-27.

took a nosedive and were replaced with a nagging doubt and insecurity that has remained.

The opening words of Paul's epistles, *grace* and *peace*, are not perfunctory words. The word order is as important as the dependent relationship they reflect—no grace, no peace. God's free grace assures us of His acceptance, our identity as His children, and our secure future with Him. Any view of assurance that is based on performance cannot do this. Instead, when performance is emphasized, stifling legalism and the guilt it produces seeps into one's psyche and into one's church.

In Our Love for God and Others

Only unconditional acceptance allows us to enjoy deeper intimacy and trust in another person, including God. When we know that we are His forever, we are free to make ourselves vulnerable as is required for any love to deepen. We can be honest and authentic without having to impress or pretend. We will never have to wonder if the relationship is secure or whether we will be rejected. The experience of being loved unconditionally is perhaps the highest human pleasure. By this experience of unconditional love, we are better motivated and equipped to keep the foremost commandment Jesus left us, to love one another. The nature of *agapē* love is to desire the best for another. When we love God, we live as He desires and treat others lovingly.

In Death

As many pastors will attest, it is difficult to officiate the funeral of an unbeliever. On the other hand, it is a certain kind of joy (mixed with sorrow) to bury someone who was a Christian and knew it. I once pastored a weak, elderly woman who had to have open heart surgery. Before the procedure, I prayed with her, and as they wheeled her off to the operating room, she pointed her skinny finger toward the ceiling and whispered, "If I don't make it, I'll see you in heaven." I didn't think she would make it, and she didn't. At her funeral service, I was able to share with joy and confidence her testimony and her assurance. Like Stephen (in Acts 7), she faced death boldly because she was certain of her eternal destiny.

How sad to think of those who die with doubts caused by overdone introspection about their faith, repentance, or level of commitment. I also feel sorry for their loved ones who might believe in performance-based assurance if the departed was not quite living for the Lord or died of suicide, yet at some level had professed faith in and lived for Jesus Christ.

What gives us confidence in "the valley of the shadow of death"? Not last minute introspection about whether we have truly believed, or whether we have been fruitful enough in life to prove we are saved—only the assurance that we are certainly saved.

In Our Service

When someone lives in the light of God's free grace, enjoying full assurance, there is joy and confidence in serving God and others. I can freely commit everything to God or make any sacrifice, because I know that it will be worth it—I am sure of my salvation and therefore my future and reward in eternity is secure. I do not serve God to prove my salvation, but to express my love and gratitude for His salvation.

When a certain missions professor visited our church, someone asked if he was afraid to travel to a country that was a dangerous place at the time. He replied simply, "I'm invincible until God is finished with me." I have had to minister in unstable and unsafe overseas situations. What gives me the confidence to go is the fact that ultimately, nothing bad can happen to me because my eternal future is secure. But my testimony pales in comparison to what I hear from the pastors and believers in other countries who have suffered every kind of persecution, yet they boldly serve God because they are sure of their eternal destiny. I cannot imagine ministering in these places with doubts about my salvation or sharing a so-called gospel of doubt with others.

It is likely that some are motivated to serve God by a sense of obligation, legalism, or even guilt. They may be living up to someone else's expectations of what they should be doing with their lives, or perhaps they have a faulty view of service as a way to assure themselves of salvation. How much better to serve God because we want to express our love and gratitude to Him for all that He has secured for us.

A longtime friend became a Christian shortly before I did. He went to Bible school and into Christian ministry influenced by Arminian theology; he believed a Christian could lose salvation. Later, circumstances in his life caused him to reconsider the significance of God's grace, and he came to understand that grace was absolutely free and unlimited. He told me, "I've been in ministry for over thirty years, but I have never ministered with joy until now." He serves God with a new attitude that is free from performance-based acceptance.

In Our Personal Practice of Godliness.

The Free Grace view of the gospel and assurance motivates me to live for God because I love Him, and I am grateful to Him; therefore, I want to serve Him. To serve Him means I cannot serve myself. I must deny myself—my own desires, ambitions, sins, and pleasures, which I gladly do. But not always. When I sin, however, I do not question my salvation; I avail myself of His abundant grace. I confess my sin and receive His forgiveness—not so I can be sure of my salvation, but so I can stay in fellowship with God. I want to live a godly life, because the reward is the relationship with God that is enhanced by obedience (cf. John 14:21). I know that God has accepted me in spite of my sin. The Free Grace view of assurance motivates me to godliness as I enjoy His love with confidence, joy, and peace.

Views that Undermine Full Assurance

Free grace and absolute full assurance are not possible with some theological systems. Three theologies in particular deny the Free Grace view of assurance.

Arminianism

This theological perspective emphasizes man's will in salvation such that a person can lose his or her salvation by sinning or by ceasing to believe. Arminians sometimes disagree on what sins or how many sins lead to loss of salvation, but even if salvation is lost only by total apostasy, this must always remain a future possibility. If the possibility remains, then absolute assurance is impossible. Arminians can only claim a present assurance of present salvation, but not a present assurance of future salvation.

Reformed Calvinism

Since this theology emphasizes God's will in our salvation, He gives us the faith to believe and that divine faith will not fail but will cause one to persevere in faithfulness and good works until the end of one's life.

Therefore, if a person does not persevere or show evidence of a changed life, that person must not be saved. With these conditions, absolute assurance is impossible. Reformed Calvinists believe in "once saved, always saved," but they cannot be sure they were once saved. Their view of assurance is that it is not absolute and not based solely on God's Word.

One Reformed Calvinist scholar, author, and pastor, Michael Eaton, has nevertheless departed from this traditional Reformed view of tentative assurance and now testifies of his full assurance. Comparing Arminianism with Calvinism, Eaton says,

> In the one case awareness of sin threatens the Arminian's confidence about continuance in the faith; in the other case awareness of sin threatens confidence about the reality of salvation. Again one notes how the developed form of Reformed thinking has a tendency to introspection.

He goes on:

> Is it not a fact of history that the Calvinist has tended to have less assurance of salvation than the Arminian? The Arminian is at least sure of their present salvation. As the result of the high-Calvinist doctrine the Calvinist often doubts their present salvation and thus has a less contented frame of mind than their evangelical Arminian friend.[49]

Lordship Salvation

This view, which defines saving faith as that which submits to Jesus Christ as Master of all of one's life, is found in both Calvinist and Arminian soteriology. Because it is based on the merit or evidence of one's submission and commitment to Christ and turning from sins, it falls into the category of performance-based assurance. Works and a changed life become necessary proof of one's submission to the Lordship of Christ. In my book on Lordship Salvation, I show how it conflicts with salvation by grace through faith alone in Christ alone and consequently, assurance.[50]

The common element in these views that undermine assurance is an emphasis on one's performance—assurance depends on a heart-felt repentant faith, commitment, faithfulness, fruit, conduct, and perseverance. In

---

[49] Eaton, *No Condemnation*, pp. 28-29. I highly recommend his book, based on his Ph.D. dissertation on Galatians, to our Reformed friends.

[50] Bing, *Lordship Salvation*. I discuss over sixty Bible passages used by Lordship Salvation adherents under the topics of faith, repentance, lordship, and discipleship.

these views, there is always something more to be done before assurance is realized. In the biblical view of salvation and assurance, grace has accomplished it all for us—"It is finished!" We are assured when we rest in that objective fact.

Some Pastoral Lessons

I served in pastoral ministry for over twenty-five years before I transitioned into another ministry. As I counseled people about many issues, I found that only the Free Grace view of the gospel frees people to have full assurance, share the gospel with confidence, and grow in Christ into maturity. Here are four things I have learned.

The Full Assurance of Free Grace Theology Gives Christians Peace

I'll never forget what one Indian man said to me the second morning of our conference on the gospel of grace (in India). He told me, "When I attended the conference yesterday, I didn't know if I would like it. But after understanding God's grace, I went home and slept in peace." I wondered how he had slept before!

On the other hand, performance-based theology unsettles people with uncertainty. This is especially true for introspective, sensitive, and earnest Christians. Asking these Christians, who testify to having believed in Jesus Christ as their Savior, to examine their faith or conduct can have a devastating spiritual effect. The sad reality is that often the most earnest and sincere Christians, when pushed to introspection, are the people who suffer with doubts and insecurity about their salvation.[51]

A woman who was in our church, whom I knew well and who had a clear testimony about her faith in Jesus Christ as her Savior, began attending a certain women's Bible study which was not part of our church. The group watched videos of a dynamic woman teacher who strongly taught Lordship Salvation (not under that designation). In the videos I watched, this teacher constantly challenges the women to question their salvation if they were not totally committed to Christ. After almost every Bible study, this introspective woman would call me with the same lament, "I don't know if I am a Christian, because I don't think I am committed to

---

[51] See Frank B. Minirth, "The Psychological Effects of Lordship Salvation," *Journal of the Grace Evangelical Society* 6:11 (Autumn 1993): 39-51.

Christ like that teacher says." To bring her back to peace and assurance, I would have to go over the gospel with her and ask her if she was trusting in Jesus Christ for eternal life. She would return to assurance when she was reminded of the scriptural promises and the fact that she was trusting in Jesus Christ alone as her only hope of eternal salvation.

I know a man who entered seminary for the sole purpose of finding out if he was saved. He was mired in introspection. (I asked him once if he was introspective, to which he answered, "Charlie, I could draw you a map of my psyche.") He is now in ministry because of his Free Grace understanding of salvation.

Contrary to the charges of some who say that we who believe in Free Grace give false assurance to people living in sin,[52] in my observation, nothing could be further from the truth. Like many Free Grace teachers that I know, my first approach to anyone who is in sin or in doubt about his salvation is never to assume he is saved, but to go over the gospel: Who is Jesus Christ, what did He provide, and what did He promise? Then I review the only requirement for salvation: Do you believe in Him as your Savior from sin who will give you eternal life as He promised? And to clarify the point, I might ask, "Have you thanked Jesus Christ for giving you the gift of eternal life?" Because of the truth of Scripture, I can make no other demands without corrupting the gospel. I do not tell him he needs to repent, because I believe that repentance, defined biblically, is a change of mind or heart. Those who believe in Christ as their Savior are changing their minds about something. Obviously, they recognize their sinful condition and separation from God—that is why they know they need to be saved. But they may also need to change their mind about Who Christ is, what He has provided, or what He promises them.[53] If I am satisfied with the answers to my questions, I can assume, for all practical purposes, that the person is born again. At that point, I can begin to deal with his sins biblically. That would include love, compassion, forgiveness, and gentleness, but also rebuke, exhortation, and reminders of God's discipline in this life and possible forfeiture of rewards here and in eternity. It

---

[52] Grudem, *"Free Grace" Theology*, see chapter 3, but especially p. 77. I do not understand the concern of Reformed Calvinists who say that Free Grace advocates give people false assurance that will send them to hell when Calvinists teach a view of election that makes those people's salvation or condemnation predetermined by God, and not affected by their view of assurance. It is hardly fair to blame Free Grace theology!

[53] The words *repent* or *repentance* are not used in the Gospel of John, a book chiefly written to bring people to eternal salvation (John 20:31). The word *repentance* is used only once in Romans (a book that explains the gospel), but not in the section on justification. The words are not used in Galatians, which is also devoted to explaining the gospel. For a fuller discussion, see Bing, *Lordship Salvation*, pp. 63-96.

is not simply a matter of questioning his salvation and sharing the gospel again. That would make church discipline and personal ministry to sinning Christians a moot point.

The Full Assurance of Free Grace Theology Allows for Confident Evangelism

Those who understand the free grace of God have confidence when presenting the gospel because they know that salvation by grace through faith in Jesus Christ is grounded in the promises of God in His Word. They can tell people that they can know they are saved based on the testimony of God (cf. 1 John 5:11-13). They can tell people who believe in Jesus that they are saved eternally, not placed on probation pending their future conduct and their turning from all sin.

When we think of the God of all grace Who has done everything He could to save us, paid the highest price He could pay for us, and desires all the world (by which I mean all human beings, not just an elect few) to be saved, we have to assume that He wants His message of salvation to be clear, simple, and accessible (not complex, complicated, or hard). Sadly, an unclear gospel based on performance or merit hinders God's desire. We would have to share a gospel of doubt and uncertainty, giving people an elusive or non-existent assurance that God accepts them.

As I said earlier, anyone who has been saved has been saved by a gospel of free grace appropriated through faith alone. But because of mankind's natural aversion to grace, many saved people begin to add other conditions to the gospel. It is like scalping tickets to an event that were obtained for free, or like hazing to make membership in a fraternity more difficult for others. How God must grieve at the impediments placed on His good news!

The Full Assurance of Free Grace Theology Frees People from Legalism

There are different forms of legalism, but basically, it is any view that adds unbiblical conditions for acceptance with God. Legalism in relationship to the gospel is the attitude that I can do something to earn, keep, or prove my salvation. By its very nature, legalism exalts the legalist and diminishes the glory due to God.

In my estimation, most of the Christian world is living in *legalism*. What I mean is that it is common to find a gospel in which something must be done (other than believing) to gain eternal life, deserve eternal life, keep eternal life, or prove eternal life. This is true about Christianity in America, but even more so in other countries.

Before I teach pastors and Bible students in other countries about the gospel, I often give them a *Gospel Survey*. It asks the question, "What must a person do to receive eternal life (be saved, become a Christian)?" It then lists eleven things commonly used as conditions for salvation. The only answer I am looking for is "Believe in Jesus Christ as Saviour from sin." Never have I surveyed a group of pastors in Africa, India, or Southeast Asia where more than 5% answered correctly. They usually choose an average of four or five things that must be done.[54]

But when we teach the gospel using the Gospel of John, Romans, Galatians, and lessons in theology, the lights come on. We see new attitudes, excitement, joy, and smiles. I have had Africans jump out of their seats with joy, and Indian pastors stand to shout and applaud their eternal security and new found assurance. This may sound extreme, but you must understand that in almost all of these places preaching typically beats people down with guilt, doubts, and the constant threat of hell. Professing Christians live in fear and uncertainty because their pastors live in fear and uncertainty. I am convinced that many of these pastors find salvation for the first time when they understand God's free grace. At the end of one week of training, a pastor stood up and shared,

> For twenty years I preached to my church congregation that they were going to hell—and I myself thought I was going to hell! Since I heard about the gospel of grace, I now know I am saved and going to heaven.

When people understand the full assurance that is possible from salvation by grace through faith alone in Christ alone, a new culture of love and acceptance develops. They also learn to handle sinning Christians in

---

[54] These results are from groups that have not previously heard Free Grace teaching. Though not a scientific survey, it helps me know whom I'm addressing. View and download the *Gospel Survey* at http://www.gracelife.org/resources/Gospel_Survey.pdf. Last accessed September 24th, 2016.

a biblical way.[55] People are freed from needless doubts, guilt, and judgmental attitudes. They rejoice in the assurance only free grace can bring.[56]

Since legalism is a constant tendency of the human psyche, we have to remind people constantly of the grace that saves and that the same grace is the chief principle of the Christian life. This means we guard them against the harmful influences of Arminianism, Reformed Calvinism, and Lordship Salvation, because these systems draw the focus from Jesus Christ and His Word to oneself. These systems diminish the gospel.

The Full Assurance of Free Grace Theology Provides the Best Basis for Christian Maturity

I have already discussed how full assurance of salvation is the best foundation for the Christian's growth and maturity. No one can go forward confidently if he is plagued with doubts about the most important thing—his own salvation.

When I was asked to write discipleship materials for new and growing Christians, I surveyed many resources, most of which had a topical "checklist" approach to discipleship. In other words, if you do these things (Bible study, devotions, prayer, witnessing, etc.) you will be a disciple, and even get a certificate that says so. Not much, if anything, was said about the motivation for making the commitments of discipleship, which may be why so many who take the training do not continue in a godly lifestyle. However, we know that if someone is properly motivated, he will find a way to grow as a disciple. As I pondered and prayed about how to write discipleship material that was biblical and included motivations for godly living, I "discovered" the book of Romans. I observed that it uses the word *grace* more than any other New Testament book (twenty-eight times), then explains the gospel progressing from sin to salvation, sanctification, security, selection (chaps 1–11), and service (chap 12). *I saw that no specific commands for Christian duty (discipleship) are given until*

---

[55] Church discipline and a ministry of restoration are irrelevant if we assume sinning people are unsaved. Instead, they should be evangelized, but that is not what is prescribed by Jesus Christ or the New Testament authors (cf. Matt 18:15-17; Gal 6:1).

[56] Wayne Grudem says professing Christians lack joy and enthusiasm about the Bible and prayer or no longer go to church because "they have never truly repented of their sins" and because Free Grace advocates have given them false assurance of salvation (*"Free Grace" Theology*, pp. 78, 97, 142). I think the problem is more likely that they do not know when they have repented enough and thus have been living with no assurance. Since most churches, in my observation, teach a performance-based assurance, it is hardly convincing that Free Grace teaching has corrupted them.

chapter 12! For eleven chapters, Paul tells the readers what God had done for them by His grace, who they have become by His grace, and how they can be secure and sure by His grace. Then he breaks out into worship (Rom 11:33-36) and begins a discussion about how they can serve God in a committed life (Rom 12:1ff.). Paul motivates his readers by reminding them what grace has done for them. I saw this same pattern in his epistles to the Galatians, Ephesians, and Colossians in which the readers are assured of the blessings and the position they possess in Christ before they are exhorted to godly conduct. I wrote my workbook on discipleship based on the book of grace, Romans.[57]

Grace, free unconditional grace that magnifies the gospel, is the best and biblical motivation for godly living.

Conclusion

To address the central theme of this book, this chapter has argued that the Free Grace view of full assurance of salvation magnifies the gospel and is the only biblical basis for godly living. Any performance-based system or theology inherently diminishes the gospel and undermines Christian maturity. And it is unbiblical, even anti-biblical. If I have to do anything more than believe, then God has not done enough for me. It is not finished—I am on probation. Eternal salvation is then conditioned on my performance either at the front end of the gospel (how I first accept it), or at the back end of the gospel (how I behave later).

The issue of assurance of salvation is crucial for godly living. Yet many do not enjoy full assurance for a number of reasons, not the least of which is the teaching that they can only know they are saved by examining their faith, repentance, good works, or commitment to Christ.

But absolute assurance is possible because it is based on the veracity of God's Word, the unconditional nature of grace, and the inherent nature of faith as certainty. The New Testament authors assume that those who believe in Christ are saved and therefore they exhort their readers to grow in Him. Turning from sins and doing good works are commanded and important, but they cannot offer full assurance because of the subjective nature of introspection and quantifying conduct. The doubts that develop from these futile efforts hinder confident Christian growth and godliness.

---

[57] Charles C. Bing, *Living in the Family of Grace* (Burleson, TX: GraceLife Ministries, 2016). It was first published in 2003.

Only full assurance of salvation and the realization of God's amazing grace can adequately and properly motivate Christians to godly living. I have shown that this is demonstrated in the Apostle Paul's epistles, but it could be shown in other Bible authors as well. A Free Grace understanding of the gospel and assurance radically affects the Christian's attitude toward life, God, others, death, service, and personal godliness. Theological systems that distort the meaning of grace and faith rob the Christian of a joyful and full assurance. This assurance gives us personal peace, confidence in sharing the promise of the gospel, protection from legalism, and the only foundation for Christian maturity.

I invite those who have doubts about their eternal destiny to search again the Scriptures. Read without prejudice the work of Jesus Christ on the cross and in His resurrection, His promises of eternal life in John, and the theology of the gospel in Romans or Galatians. Do you believe what God says? Take your eyes off of yourself and put them on the Savior! Your life will be changed forever for the better.

I invite those who disagree theologically to examine again the Scriptures in their context and allow God's Word to speak undressed by tradition, creeds, confessions, and commentators. I challenge you to examine yourselves as to what you are trusting in for eternal salvation—the ideas of men, your own repentance, your good works, or the immutable promise of God in His Word that says whoever simply believes in the Lord Jesus Christ as Savior has eternal life.

If you have believed in Christ, the God of all grace wants you to know and rejoice that you are His forever. *Soli Deo gloria.*

FREE GRACE EXALTS CHRIST AND HIS WORK

By Roger Fankhauser

In the realm of Christian theology in all its various forms, Free Grace theology uniquely exalts Christ. Every other Christian system boils down to Christ *plus* something. Sometimes, the "plus something" relates to our initial salvation (e.g., faith in Christ *plus* baptism or faith in Christ *plus* being good). Sometimes it relates to our security (e.g., faith in Christ *plus* continuing in faith and/or producing good works to avoid losing our salvation). Sometimes it relates to our assurance (faith in Christ *plus* evident external works to confirm that we truly believed). In each of these other views, some focus is taken off Christ—albeit unintentionally—and placed on us.[1] Some claim Free Grace underemphasizes trusting in Christ as a person.[2] However, Free Grace alone keeps an undivided focus on Christ, whether considering someone's initial salvation,[3] his growth as a believer, security, assurance, reward at the Bema, or glorification.

Free Grace, in all its various forms, universally holds four key theological assertions:

(1) Initial salvation comes by grace alone through faith alone in Christ alone.

(2) On the cross, Jesus Christ paid the price in full for our sins and was raised from the dead.

---

[1] All the various systems claim to exalt Christ. Many proclaim salvation by faith alone in Christ alone. Thus, they would likely take issue with the statement that they take some of the focus off of Christ. However, to the degree that we look at our own works, even if only for assurance, we do, in fact, detract from a Christ alone perspective.

[2] Grudem, *"Free Grace" Theology*, pp. 105-107, 142.

[3] For purposes of this chapter, *initial salvation* refers to all that God does on our behalf the moment we believe in Christ, including, among other things, justification (being declared righteous).

(3) The believer's security and assurance are based solely on the objective truth of Christ's work on the cross, the promises of Scripture (such as John 3:16), and the faithfulness of God.

(4) Good works should result in the life of a believer, but such works cannot serve as the logical basis for one's security or assurance. Works provide far too subjective a basis for such an evaluation. Logically, such a system detracts from the person and work of Christ.[4]

A Word about Theology, Logic, and Life

The phrase "logical basis" points out the important connection between logic and theology. "Logic may be defined as the science that evaluates arguments."[5] Theological arguments, such as those in this chapter, are not immune to logical analysis. Sound theological conclusions require both solid exegesis and sound logical argumentation.[6] The *content* of a theological argument may sound convincing, but the rules of logic, applied to the format and wording of the argument, may render it unsound.

For example, does logic support the conclusion that good works or life change give valid evidence of the reality of someone's salvation? The structure of the argument looks something like this:[7]

(1) An individual can have confidence in the reality of his salvation by examining the evidence of his good works or change in his life if and only if the person has an objective standard for that evaluation.

---

[4] It is true that good works can and do glorify God, and that Free Grace, properly understood, promotes such good works. But when these works become part of the evaluation of whether or not someone *really* believed, the focus moves from Christ alone to Christ plus the life of the believer.

[5] Patrick Hurley, *A Concise Introduction to Logic*, 7th ed. (Belmont, CA: Wadsworth/Thomson, 2000), p. 1.

[6] A sound logical argument is one in which every premise is true and is valid, that is, it contains no logical fallacies. A fallacy may be a structural fallacy or an informal fallacy, such as *ad hominem*, straw man, or any one of many such fallacies. (*Ibid.*, pp. 46-50.)

[7] The content-blind form of the argument looks like this:
X, if and only if Y
Not Y
Therefore, Not X.
"If and only if" means the condition(s) that follow are necessary for the first term to be true.
"Not Y" means that Y is false, which renders X false as well ("Not X").

(2) No objective standard exists.[8]

(3) Therefore, an individual *cannot* have confidence in the reality of his salvation based on this examination.

The logic applies whether one looks positively at the existence of fruit as evidence that someone is indeed saved or at sin (especially habitual sins) as evidence that he is not saved. No objective standard exists to evaluate the difference between a believer's sin or pattern of sin (1 John 1:10) and that of someone who thinks he is a believer but is not. Thus, the logic of either argument can only lead to uncertainty about the reality of one's conversion, even when used in conjunction with other evidences.[9]

Language matters in arguments. Words convey two dimensions of meaning: Cognitive (conveying information) and emotive (expressing or evoking meanings).[10] Most words have more than one cognitive meaning, and if an incorrect meaning is used by the one making the argument or assumed by the one evaluating the argument, the soundness of the argument comes into question. The words *assurance* and *good works* in the above argument serve as prime examples in which clear definitions are critical.

Logic and life don't always align. People do not always act consistently with the logical conclusions of their positions, regardless of their theological system. When an appeal to logic is used in this chapter, it means, "logical consistency within this system would lead to this conclusion." It does *not* mean that all who hold the theological position under discussion actually hold to the logical conclusion.

The Starting Point—The Work of the Trinity

Ephesians 1 provides one of the most theologically rich passages in the Bible, describing the work of the Trinity on behalf of our salvation. Paul

---

[8] Of course, the Bible is an objective standard. It does objectively define sin and righteousness, so an individual can determine if a specific action is sinful or not. It does not, however, define how much sin gives evidence that one never believed or how many good works are enough to give evidence that one has done enough to have confidence in his salvation.

[9] Despite his repeated appeal to evaluate one's life to determine whether one is saved, Grudem cites the Westminster Confession (18.1-2) and concludes that "[H]istoric Protestantism has taught that believers may attain an 'infallible' assurance of salvation and have 'certainty' that 'they are in the state of grace'" (Grudem, *"Free Grace" Theology*, p. 96).

[10] Grudem appears to use the word *just* for its emotive power when he writes, "The first Free Grace definition of *repentance*…claims that *repentance* means just a 'change of mind' (and not any internal resolve to turn from sin)." The cognitive meaning is correct, but the emotive meaning minimizes the view (Grudem, *"Free Grace" Theology*, p. 55).

uses each of two phrases, with slight variations, three times in this section; each phrase in connection with the work of each person of the Trinity: "According to his purpose" (1:5, 9, 11),[11] and "to the praise of his glory" (1:6, 12, 14).[12]

The focus of the work of all three persons of the Trinity is Jesus Christ. The Father "blessed us in Christ with every spiritual blessing," "chose us in him [Christ]," and "predestined us for adoption to himself as sons through Jesus Christ," all "according to the purpose of his [the Father's] will, to the praise of his glorious grace [better, 'the praise of his glory'] with which he has blessed us in the Beloved" (Eph 1:3-6). The Father's work also includes sealing the believer with the Holy Spirit in Christ ("In him you also…were sealed with the promised Holy Spirit," 1:13). The Spirit is described as "the guarantee of our inheritance until we acquire possession of it, to the praise of his glory" (1:14). Based on the work of Christ every believer receives "redemption through his blood, the forgiveness of our trespasses," and the inheritance guaranteed by the Holy Spirit (1:7-12).

No theological system denies the Christological emphasis in this passage. Of course, this passage contains some difficult theological issues (e.g., "chose us," "predestined," "works all things according to the council of his will"), but regardless of one's theological leanings, it is impossible to deny that the focal point of this passage is the person and work of Jesus Christ.

Paul adds that we have this redemption and forgiveness "according to the *riches*[13] of his grace, which he *lavished*[14] upon us" (vv 7-8). These superlatives emphasize the greatness of God's grace, which flows from

---

[11] The variations are, "according to the purpose of his will," (v 5), "according to his purpose," (v 9), and "according to the purposes of him," (v 11). However, the Greek word translated "purpose" in v 11 (*prothesis*) is different from the other two verses (*eudokia*). The former term refers to "that which is planned or purposed in advance," (Louw and Nida, *Greek-English Lexicon of the New Testament*, s.v. *prothesis*); the latter refers to "that which pleases someone" (*ibid.*, s.v. *eudokia*). Some translations distinguish the two terms by translating *eudokia* as "kind intention" (e.g., NASB).

[12] The variations are "to the praise of his glorious grace" (v 6), and "to the praise of his glory" (v 12 and v 14). Each phrase in the Greek contains the structure *eis epainon doxēs autou*. Translations differ on the wording of verse 6. For example, the ESV and NIV translate it "to the praise of his glorious grace," while the NASB, NKJV, and NET translate it "to the glory of his grace." Both options are possible, but the latter seems preferable as it maintains the parallel structure of the three verses ("to the praise of his glory…").

[13] "Riches" translates *ploutos*, meaning, "a high point on any scale and having the implication of value as well as abundance—'great, abundant, abundantly, greatly, extremely" (Louw and Nida, s.v. *ploutos*) The word is used 22 Times in the New Testament, 5 in Ephesians, and is translated "riches" or "wealth."

[14] "[T]o cause something to exist in an abundance—'to provide in abundance, to provide a great deal of, to cause to be abundant.'" (Louw and Nida, s.v. *perisseuō*).

Him towards the believer. A person becomes the recipient of this grace simply and immediately when he believes in Jesus Christ, just as Paul said happened to the Ephesians: "In him ['the Lord Jesus,' v 13] you also, when you heard the word of truth, the gospel of your salvation, and believed in him, were sealed with the promised Holy Spirit" (Eph 1:13). Paul concisely defined this gospel message in 1 Cor 15:3-4:[15]

> For I delivered to you as of first importance what I also received:
> that Christ died for our sins in accordance with the Scriptures,
> that he was buried, that he was raised on the third day in accor-
> dance with the Scriptures.

To appropriate the promised results of God's grace (our initial salvation), the required response to this simple message is equally simple, "Believe in Him."[16] Thus far, no system—Reformed, Arminian, Free-Grace, or any other that teaches "salvation by faith in Christ"—would disagree with the premise that the gospel exalts Christ and His work. However, problems arise with the way other systems address sanctification, security, and assurance.

Security and Assurance

How a person understands the connection between initial salvation and the security of a believer impacts his understanding of assurance which, in turn, impacts his motives for living as a believer. Only Free Grace avoids the logical pitfall of including the believer's ongoing faith and/or his works in defining security and assurance.

Two views exist among those who believe a person can lose his salvation. One view holds that "loss of faith" results in a person losing salvation. This view argues that a person is saved by faith, but God honors man's free will so that, should a person cease to believe in Jesus, he forfeits salvation. A second view argues that a person who habitually sins or commits a serious enough sin loses his or her salvation. I once played golf with a pastor who held a *loss of salvation* view. Upon losing his temper following a particularly frustrating hole, he asked to be excused for a moment

---

[15] He includes all the elements of the gospel in Ephesians, but the succinct wording of this passage makes clear the message Paul proclaimed throughout his ministry (1 Cor 15:11, in which *preach* is in the present tense, emphasizing that this message was not limited to the Corinthians).

[16] Many add "repent," so that the required response becomes "repent and believe." It is beyond the scope of this chapter to discuss biblical repentance and how it fits within Free Grace theology. However, even those who say the response is "repent and believe" do not deny the necessity of faith alone in Christ alone.

so he could get re-saved. I thought he was joking, but he was not. While this may be an extreme example, it demonstrates the belief that, according to this system, one's behavior can result in loss of salvation. In both of these views, the logical position is that the believer's security depends on the work of Christ *plus* the faithfulness or holiness of the individual. As a result, no one holding this view can logically have full assurance of his salvation since no person can guarantee he won't fall into sin at some time in the future or that some crisis in life won't cause him to lose his faith.

On the other hand, Reformed theology argues that a person cannot lose his salvation. However, it also argues that habitual sin implies that the person did not *truly* believe. It also argues that a believer will necessarily produce externally evident good works as evidence that the person truly believed. Thus, although this view argues for the security of the true believer, assurance requires evaluation of both a person's works and his sins. It is not unusual for people within this system who struggle with sin to conclude: "I must not really be saved since I cannot overcome this sin." And in my case, I remember as a young believer wondering if I had produced enough fruit to prove I was really saved.

Reformed theologian Wayne Grudem describes his view of the relationship between assurance and works:

> Therefore, the proper answer to the question "How many good works does one have to do in order to be assured of salvation?" is, "Some." To be more specific *some* change of life gives a basis for *some* measure of assurance, and a greater change of life gives a basis for a stronger assurance…God alone knows with absolute certainty everyone who is saved and everyone who is lost, for "the Lord knows those who are his" (2 Tim. 2:19), but we can perceive stronger or weaker outward indications of what is actually in someone's heart, both our own hearts and those of others.[17]

He also correctly assesses the logical similarities between the *loss of salvation* view and the *not really saved* view concerning the sinning professor of faith in Christ:

> [I]n terms of pastoral care with those who have strayed away from their Christian profession, we should realize that *Calvinists and Arminians* (those who believe in the perseverance of the saints and those who think that Christians can lose their salvation) *will both counsel a "backslider" in the same way.* According

---

[17] Grudem, *"Free Grace" Theology*, p. 92. Emphasis his.

to the Arminian this person was a Christian at one time but is no longer a Christian. According to the Calvinist, such a person never really was a Christian in the first place and is not one now. But in both cases the biblical counsel given would be the same: "You do not appear to be a Christian now—you must repent of your sins and trust in Christ for your salvation!" Though the Calvinist and Arminian would differ on their interpretation of the previous history, they would agree on what should be done in the present.[18]

In a footnote, he adds:

Of course, both the Calvinist and the Arminian would allow for the possibility that the "backslidden" person is truly born again and had just fallen into sin and doubt. But both would agree that it is pastorally wise to assume that the person is not a Christian until some evidence of present faith is forthcoming.[19]

Thus, both camps detract from *Christ alone* in their views of assurance by including examination and evaluation of one's works as a necessary part of a person's assurance. Such examination and evaluation is necessarily subjective. To the degree that someone bases his assurance on his works, he moves from a God-centered, grace-based perspective of his security to a man-centered, performance-based perspective. Free Grace, on the other hand, holds that both the believer's security and assurance are based entirely on God's promises and work. As such, Free Grace exalts Christ and His work in this important dimension of our salvation.

The following small sampling of typical New Testament passages affirms that Jesus paid the price in full for our sin so that the believer's initial salvation results from faith alone in Christ alone: "For God so loved the world, that he gave his only Son, that whoever believes in him should not perish but have eternal life" (John 3:16). And, "For by grace you have been saved through faith. And this is not your own doing; it is the gift of God, not a result of works, so that no one may boast" (Eph 2:8-9). And, "Truly, truly, I say to you, whoever hears my word and believes him who sent me has eternal life. He does not come into judgment, but has passed from death to life" (John 5:24).

The first two well-known verses emphasize that salvation (receiving eternal life) comes as a gift from God upon belief in Jesus. The third verse reinforces that a person receives eternal life by faith alone, adding

---

[18] Grudem, *Systematic Theology*, p. 806. Emphasis his.

[19] *Ibid.*, p. 806, fn 29.

the important detail that the believer "has passed from death to life." The Greek term for "passed" is in the perfect tense, which emphasizes a permanent state in the present. In other words, once a person "has passed from death to life," his position has changed permanently. The believer permanently escapes judgment and death (here describing his spiritual state, not the escape of physical death). These verses, along with many similar passages, emphasize that the believer's security is based solely on the work of God. Ephesians 1:3-14, previously addressed, makes the same point with its emphasis on the work of the Trinity regarding our salvation.

Passages such as these are promises made by God, revealed to us in His Word. When a person takes the promises of God and personalizes them, he or she is trusting God's faithfulness to honor those promises. Since Scripture reveals the faithfulness of God (e.g., Num 23:19, Deut 7:9, Ps 36:5, 1 Cor 10:13), this confidence has a sure basis. Thus, God gives salvation—which is based entirely on the work of Christ—and because of His faithfulness, guarantees the believer's eternal destiny. Thus, assurance is based on the objective truth of the work of the Father, Son, and Holy Spirit on behalf of believers, on the objective truth of God's Word that promises salvation to any and all who believe in Christ for eternal life, and on the objective faithfulness of God to keep His promises.

But wait…does this mean the Scriptures offer assurance to the disobedient believer?

Yes, because our security and assurance are not based on our faithfulness, but God's.

> The saying is trustworthy, for:
>
> If we have died with him, we will also live with him;
>
> if we endure, we will also reign with him;
>
> if we deny him, he also will deny us;
>
> if we are faithless, he remains faithful—for he cannot deny himself. (2 Tim 2:11-13)

"To encourage Timothy further to endure hardship, Paul cited a commonly accepted and used quotation that encouraged believers to remain faithful to their Christian profession."[20] The first pair of "if" statements deal with a positive situation; the second pair deal with a negative situation. The first statement gives a promise for every believer (those who have "died with him") that they will "live with him" (future tense). The second

---

[20] Tom Constable, *Tom Constable's Expository Notes on the Bible* (Galaxie Software, 2003), 2 Tim 2:10.

statement ("if we endure we will also reign with him [future tense]"), gives a promise of future reward for faithful believers.

That "reign with him" and "live with him" are not synonymous is clear by the verb tenses. "Died" is in the past tense.[21] Paul uses the phrase "died with Christ" as a synonym for our new relationship with Christ when we come to faith in Him (Rom 6:8; Col 2:20; 3:3). Thus, it speaks of our initial salvation which guarantees that we will live with Him. "Endure," however, is in the present tense, emphasizing something in the present life experience of the person. Enduring happens in a different time frame than dying. "Died" is an initial salvation issue; "endure" is a sanctification issue. Thus, these first two "if" statements deal with the *unconditional* promise of life with Him and the *conditional* prospect of reigning with Him (reward).

The next two "if" statements, however, deal with negative situations in the life of a believer. "Deny him" is in the future tense, implying it is not something going on in the present, but it is a real future possibility. The one enduring now may well become one who denies Him later. The one who denies Christ is denied (also future tense) by Christ. That brings into question, "In what way does Christ deny the believer who denies Him?" Two options are (1) He denies this person entrance into heaven (that is, either the person loses his salvation or he was never truly saved) or (2) He denies this person at the Bema seat "so that each one [believer] may receive what is due for what he has done in the body, whether good or evil" (2 Cor 5:10b). The first option contradicts the first promise that the one who has died with Him will also live with Him. The fourth "if" also contradicts this option: "If we are faithless, he remains faithful—for he cannot deny himself." Thus, the only denial a believer could face is denial of reward at the Bema, specifically, being denied the role of reigning with Him.

This final "if" statement deserves a bit more consideration. Those who hold that "denial" speaks of "never having been saved" or "losing one's salvation" must define the faithfulness of Christ in a unique way: He is faithful to designate him to hell as a result of his unbelief.[22] However,

---

[21] Technically, this verb is in the aorist tense. The aorist indicates undefined action which usually, but not always, occurs in the past. The meaning of the verb and the context determine whether it is a past action and whether it is a punctiliar action or not. In this case, both the context and the verb "die with him" (*sunapothnēskō*) justify translating the verb as a point action in the past.

[22] Grudem takes a different slant. He argues the word "probably does not refer to complete loss of saving faith but to a temporary weakness of faith or temporary unfaithfulness in conduct..." He says the verb here (*apisteō*) "need not imply complete unbelief, because one possible meaning is 'be unfaithful'" (Grudem, *"Free Grace" Theology*, p. 88, fn 12. The ESV, however, translates

nothing in the context demands this, unless one imports his theological system into the interpretation. If Paul's point is to encourage Timothy (and by application other believers) to endure hardship, words of comfort and encouragement carry far more weight than a threat. The threat would be, "if you don't endure, Christ will be faithful and relegate you to hell." Encouragement would be, "even if you are faithless, Christ will not deny Himself as the One who promised eternal life and gave it to you freely." This view is supported by the use of "we" throughout the section. Paul implies even he and Timothy could become faithless; yet nowhere does Paul ever express any doubt about his ultimate destiny (cf., Phil 1:21, 2 Cor 5:8).

Notice how this exalts Christ and His work. On the cross, Jesus accomplished all that was necessary to secure our salvation. He promised eternal life to any and all who believe in Him. In one of His confrontations with the Jews, Jesus spoke of His role in the security of—and therefore the assurance of salvation for—those who simply believe in Him:

> I give them eternal life, and they will never perish, and no one will snatch them out of my hand. My Father, who has given them to me, is greater than all, and no one is able to snatch them out of the Father's hand. (John 10:28-29)

Eternal life is given freely; the recipients of eternal life are told they will "never perish," Jesus holds them securely in *His* hands and the Father also holds them securely in *His* hands. Combining these words of Jesus with the words of Paul in Second Timothy, we conclude that even the faithless believer is secure in his or her faith and can have assurance that Jesus is clinging to him faithfully.

This understanding is counterintuitive. People are so performance driven that it seems impossible that a professing believer could, for any of a thousand reasons, walk away from his faith, and yet be a genuine child of God. Assuming the person believed,[23] this may be the case exactly. The

---

six of the seven occurrences of this verb outside of 2 Tim 2:13 as "do/does/did not believe" or "disbelieved." The one use that is translated "unfaithful" (Rom 3:3) can be translated "did not believe" (NASB, NKJV, NET). Thus, the understanding here of "temporary unfaithfulness" seems system driven rather than textually driven.

23   Granted, some people believe they are Christians when, in reality, they are not. However, the issue is not what they claim; the issue is, in what or in whom do they believe? John 1:12-13 makes this clear: "But to all who did receive him, who believed in his name, he gave the right to become children of God, who were born, not of blood nor of the will of the flesh nor of the will of man, but of God." Someone might mistakenly think he is a Christian because he goes to church, comes from a Christian home, walked an aisle, lives in a Christian country, etc. Thus, it is valid to ask the person who deserts his or her professed faith about his or her salvation. It is *possible* such a person never trusted Jesus. However, Free Grace theology would assert that

position of "child of God" is not dependent upon the person's behavior, but upon the greatness of God's grace and what Christ has done on his behalf.

Grace exalts Christ and His work because it recognizes that He holds on to us. Our security is completely in His hands! The person who believes in Jesus as the Son of God who died on the cross for his sins and was raised from the dead has eternal life from the moment he or she believes, even if he or she should wander later in life. However, this surely does not give a believer permission to walk away from his or her faith nor does it justify choosing to walk away from faithful living in order to more fully exalt Christ (Rom 6:1). It is not the disobedience that exalts Him; rather, His faithfulness *despite* the believer's disobedience exalts Him. It simply means that *should* a believer take this unfortunate route in life, Jesus' faithfulness trumps his or her unfaithfulness and ensures his or her ultimate destiny. This leads to two obvious questions: (1) if we are secure entirely because of Jesus' work on our behalf, why should we live faithfully, and (2) are there consequences for unfaithfulness?

Living as a Believer—Motive and Method

Of course, all systems will argue that their understanding of Christian living (sanctification) exalts Christ. But upon careful examination, it seems Free Grace theology does so to a greater degree. Here's why:

Free Grace alone fully eliminates any fear about one's salvation, any resulting fear of hell, and the need for any self-focus to evaluate one's salvation as motivations to follow Christ. There are consequences for disobedience, to be sure, but hell is not one of them. Free Grace alone places the motivation to serve completely at the feet of Jesus.

Human motives are difficult to discern. We can look at the actions of people or listen to their words and think we know their motives, but it is often not that simple. I am not always sure of my own motives, let alone someone else's. Thus, Free Grace logically allows a person to act with pure motives, but just as not all who adhere to other systems act in the way the logic of their system leads, so, too, with the person who holds to Free Grace. In practice, this person may not be moved by the motives that flow from Free Grace theology, but this does not minimize that logically, Free Grace theology provides the greatest freedom to follow Christ in the

---

deserting one's faith is not *necessarily* evidence that the person never believed or that he lost his salvation.

most Christ exalting way, free from any concern about earning, keeping, or proving a person's relationship with Him.

Many outside Free Grace circles do not see this as a plus for the believer. Those who are opposed to or don't understand Free Grace often make the accusation that it is antinomian; that is, it promotes lawlessness or living without rules. If, by this, they meant that Free Grace recognizes that the Mosaic Law has no binding impact on the believer's life, I would agree. But that is not what they mean. They mean, "Free Grace teaches the professing believer can live as he wishes, with no consequences for disobedience."

Such thinking is not new. Paul addressed this very problem in Romans 6, in which he asks the questions, "What shall we say then? Are we to continue in sin that grace may abound?" (Rom 6:1), and "What then? Are we to sin because we are not under law but under grace? By no means!" (Rom 6:15). It seems some concluded (incorrectly) that, since they were under grace, they were free to sin. The first question addresses license; the second addresses lawlessness. Both questions address faulty thinking about grace and Paul answered both with an emphatic "By no means!"[24] But in both cases Paul neither questions his readers' salvation, nor implies that they are destined for eternal separation from God should they live this way. Instead, because of the believer's identity in Christ, he answers the first question with this admonition:

> Do not present your members to sin as instruments for unrighteousness, but present yourselves to God as those who have been brought from death to life, and your members to God as instruments for righteousness. For sin will have no dominion over you, since you are not under law but under grace. (Rom 6:13-14)

And the second question with this:

> But now that you have been set free from sin and have become slaves of God, the fruit you get leads to sanctification and its end, eternal life. (Rom 6:22)

Rather than question their identity as believers, he assumes it and instead challenges their thinking about the appropriateness of sin in their

---

[24] Much of this paragraph taken from Roger Fankhauser, "Why Not Sin Like the Devil?" in *21 Tough Questions About Grace*, Hawley, ed., p. 21.

lives. Free Grace teaches that the believer does not need to do anything to earn, keep, or prove God's love.

> Most people imagine the message of Christianity runs some-thing like this: *Love the Lord, do good, give generously, live right, serve God, and the Lord will really love you and bless you.* That is not the Christian gospel! The true gospel certainly contains those three elements, but in a different sequence. Here's the biblical formula: *God really loves you and has blessed you; there-fore love the Lord, do good, give generously, live right, and serve God.*[25]

We could rewrite the first condition this way: Most people imagine the message of Christianity runs something like this: "Love the Lord, do good, give generously, live right, serve God, persevere to the end, and you will *prove* the Lord really loves you," or "Love the Lord, do good, give generously, live right, serve God, and *you will not lose* your salvation." These are the logical conclusions necessitated by other systems. Granted, those who hold to these other systems would argue that the ability to do any of these things comes only by God's power and not our own, yet the conclusion of these systems is logically inescapable: part of a believer's motivation for obedience flows from the conclusion that his obedience in some measure proves or secures his salvation.

Free Grace frees the believer from this motivation. Because the believer understands that his salvation is secure from the moment of belief, based on the work, character, and promises of God alone, he is free to serve, without fear about whether or not he is saved.

What are some of the motivators?

A Response to Grace

In Luke 7:36-50, a Pharisee invited Jesus to dine with him. A woman with a reputation (a "sinner," v 37) entered the home, wet Jesus' feet with her tears, wiped them with her hair, kissed His feet, and anointed them with ointment (v 38). The reader can almost feel the revulsion of the Pharisee as he says that if Jesus were a prophet, He would *know* that this woman was a sinner. Jesus addresses the heart of the matter with a short story of two men forgiven a financial debt, one debt ten times that of the other. He asks, "Now which of them will love him more?" (v 42b).

---

[25] Alan D. Wright, *Free Yourself, Be Yourself* (Colorado Springs: Multnomah Books, 2010), p. 35. Emphasis his.

The Pharisee answers logically, "The one forgiven the greater debt." Jesus affirmed his answer, and then chides him for failing to show acts of hospitality and love towards Him, whereas the woman had not ceased to show such acts of hospitality and love since she entered the room. He concludes with these words:

> Therefore I tell you, her sins, which are many, are forgiven—
> for she loved much. But he who is forgiven little, loves little.
> And he said to her, "Your sins are forgiven." (Luke 7:47-48)[26]

Jesus' point is not that this woman actually sinned more than the Pharisee, although her sins were more culturally unacceptable than those of the Pharisee. Instead, the issue is awareness of the extent of their sinfulness. Every person who takes a serious look at his or her sinfulness should see that he or she is a sinner by nature and by practice. All are "dead" in trespasses and sins (Eph 2:1); all are equally lost apart from Christ. Paul makes the point that "all have sinned and fall short of the glory of God" (Rom 3:23). Isaiah, in response to his experience of seeing the Lord on His throne, concluded he was ruined, undone,[27] a man of unclean lips (Isa 6:1-7). Paul and Isaiah saw the extent of their sinfulness and correspondingly, the greatness of God's grace on their behalf. Why else would the woman unashamedly worship at Christ's feet? Why would Isaiah say, "Here I am! Send me," even before his job description was given (Isa 6:8b)? Why else would Paul say:

> Indeed, I count everything as loss because of the surpassing
> worth of knowing Christ Jesus my Lord. For his sake I have
> suffered the loss of all things and count them as rubbish, in
> order that I may gain Christ. (Phil 3:8)?

One primary reason: they simply responded to the vastness of God's forgiveness and the greatness of His grace. Christ paid for it all; He gives eternal life freely with no strings attached; He holds the believer securely whether he is living rightly or not. What better motive to follow Him? Logically, Free Grace gives freedom to follow Christ simply as a response

---

[26] Editor's note: For an explanation of the word *for* in Luke 7:47, see Hawley, "Free Grace Teaches Us to Turn from Sins" in the present book, pp. 43-45.

[27] The ESV translates the Hebrew word here (*dāmâ*) as "lost," but in no other instances of the word does it do so. It is better translated "undone" or "ruined." "Among other translations in the ESV of the same verb form (*niphal*, perfect) include 'undone' and 'laid waste' (both in Isa 15:1), 'destroyed' (Hos 4:6), 'perish' (Hos 10:7), etc., which better fits the lexical definition of the verb, 'cease, cause to cease, cut off, destroy'" (Francis Brown, Samuel Rolles Driver, and Charles Augustus Briggs, *Enhanced Brown-Driver-Briggs Hebrew and English Lexicon* [Oxford, UK: Clarendon Press, 1977], s.v. *dāmâ*). The primary thought is that Isaiah recognizes both his sinfulness and the people's sinfulness in light of God's holiness.

to God's grace, without even a hint of "if you don't do this, you either weren't saved or you lost your salvation." Living rightly as a response to God's free grace exalts Christ.

A Response of Love

The story in Luke 7 alludes to love, but the focus there is a response to forgiveness. Speaking to the eleven believing disciples, Jesus more directly addresses a response of love in the Upper Room:

> "A new commandment I give to you, that you love one another: just as I have loved you, you also are to love one another." (John 13:34)

He commands these eleven to follow His example, loving others the way He loved them.[28] Later in the same discourse, He said:

> "Whoever has my commandments and keeps them, he it is who loves me. And he who loves me will be loved by my Father, and I will love him and manifest myself to him." (John 14:21, see also 14:15, 23; 1 John 5:3).

Thus, the right response to one's love for Jesus is to keep His commandments. Notice the flow: "If you love me (Jesus), you will keep my commandments." Not, "If you want me (Jesus) to love you," or "to prove I really love you," but "if you love me." Obedience here flows from a response of love towards Jesus.

An observant reader might see the phrase, "And he who loves me will be loved by my Father" and infer some sort of "obedience results in God loving me" scenario. But such a conclusion does not flow from the greater context. First, Jesus clearly taught that the gospel message flows from God's love:

> For God so loved the world, that he gave his only Son, that whoever believes in him should not perish but have eternal life. (John 3:16)

John adds in 1 John 4:19 that "We love because he first loved us." In other words, our ability to love results from God's first loving us. Thus, God's love is not something we earn. If this is true, then in what way

---

[28] The idea of love for others was not unique to the teaching of Jesus. Leviticus 19:18b says, "you shall love your neighbor as yourself: I am the LORD" (a passage frequently cited in the New Testament [Matt 19:19; 22:39; Mark 12:31; Luke 10:27; Rom 13:9; Gal 5:14; Jas 2:8]). The new aspect of the commandment lies in the words, "as I have loved you."

will the believer "be loved by my Father"? The issue in the upper room is intimacy with God, not initial salvation. Thus, when we love Jesus, we keep His commandments. By loving Him, we enter into intimacy with Jesus. And when we love Him, we experience His love for us (i.e., we experience intimacy with God), but we do not earn it. In fact, Hebrews emphasizes that even when believers are disciplined by God, He acts as a loving Father training His children. The believer is loved by God unconditionally, even when he needs discipline!

For the Glory of God

Paul concludes a discussion of debatable issues with the admonition, "So, whether you eat or drink, or whatever you do, do all to the glory of God " (1 Cor 10:31). The application clearly goes beyond debatable issues; it applies to any and all actions we take. The idea shows up in many variations in the New Testament, such as "Therefore be *imitators* of God, as beloved children" (Eph 5:1, emphasis added). Understanding God's grace, and what He has done and continues to do for us related to our salvation frees us to exalt Him in our actions with the pure motive of bringing Him glory. To the extent that we look at our own lives for assurance, we detract from His glory.

A Response from Being Secure

Being a foster parent taught me many things. One relates to the power of living in a secure home. Most foster children do not end up in the system because their home life is solid. Most of them love their parents, despite what may have gone on at home, but they learned unhealthy approaches to life in their unhealthy homes. When they enter the foster system, they don't immediately see their foster home as a wonderful home (even if the foster parents try to make it one!). Over time, they may relax in the foster home and realize it is a safe place, but there is one thing always missing: real security.

The child is a "ward of the state." As long as a child is in the foster system, he or she could get moved from his or her foster home. It could be because of his behavior, the choice of the foster parents, the decision of Child Protective Services, or a host of other circumstances. One child came to us from a home that said they wanted to adopt her, but the parents decided they could not deal with her behavior and changed their minds. Can you imagine this girl's heartache?

Sometimes the children act out to test the new parents. Sometimes the children act out because that is how they learned to survive. But such behavior never comes from feeling completely secure in the home.

Something changes, however, when a child is adopted. Granted, the child may not be aware of the difference, but it is real. When a child is adopted, a legal security changes the relationship. The foster parents do not love the child any more simply because the legal relationship changes; but the child is now permanently and legally tied to the parents. Thus, at least as much as possible in human relationships, the child no longer has to worry about whether he gets to stay in the home, even if he misbehaves (which he will!).

In a similar way, the believer is an adopted child of God (Eph 1:5). Unlike a foster child but like an adopted child, our position, properly understood, should result in great security, with confidence in our new legal relationship with God and thus a real understanding of the freedom we have in Christ.

A second lesson relates to how people change. We had a foster daughter who had a bit of a temper. She would yell and cry sometimes when she didn't get her way. Well, okay, she threw a temper tantrum! Every time, I would have a conversation with her like this:

Me: We love you, but we cannot put up with that kind of behavior. Has it ever got you what you wanted?

Her: No.

Me: Do you think it will work this time?

Her: No.

Me: Then why are you acting like this?

Her: I don't know.

She understood the logic; she experienced *not* getting what she wanted based on her behavior, yet she kept doing it. Her behavior was habitual. She didn't change after the first time we had the conversation, or the second, or the third, or... Change takes time. Her behavior parallels a "besetting sin" or a "habitual sin" that may be an issue in the life of a believer. A person on the outside, or even the person herself, might look at that ongoing, habitual sin and think, "She's not really a believer because she has this habitual sin," or "She obviously lost her salvation because of that habitual sin." However, because we are securely adopted children, even such bad behavior cannot separate us from the love of Christ. Christ is exalted, not through our behavior in this case, but despite our behavior and because of His unflinching hold on us!

Free Grace theology leads to *real* security and *real* assurance, both of which provide motivation to follow Christ with the freedom that comes when there is no fear about our ultimate destiny.

(Good news: the children in both scenarios were adopted by great families who love them!)

Following Christ Matters—Accountability

Paul reminds his readers that when they leave this earthly body, they will be clothed with an eternal body. He states that his priority, whether "home or away" (a figure of speech meaning "always"), was to be pleasing to the Lord. He then reminded his readers that every believer, including himself, is accountable for what he does in this life as a believer:

> For we [plural, all believers] must all appear before the judgment seat [Bema] of Christ, so that each one [singular, each individual believer] may receive what is due for what he has done in the body, whether good or evil. (2 Cor 5:10)

Paul includes himself in this group. Every believer gives an account resulting in "receiving what is due." This wording clearly indicates Paul is not talking about our initial salvation. That belongs to the believer by grace alone, not as the result of "what he has done in the body." What a person has done (works) has no bearing on receiving eternal life. Instead, believers will "receive" for what they have done in this life, whether what they did was good or evil (better, "worthless"). One lexicon gives this definition for the word translated "receive:"

> [T]o cause someone to experience something on the basis of what that person has already done—"to cause to experience in return, to cause to suffer for, to cause to experience in proportion to, to be repaid for."[29]

This sounds like a wage earned ("experience in return"), not something bestowed as a gift, and thus it cannot be speaking about our initial

---

[29] Louw and Nida, *Greek-English Lexicon*, s.v. *komidzō*.

salvation. This judgment of the believer at the Bema evaluates the quality of the believer's works, not his eternal destiny.[30]

Does this contradict what was said in a footnote earlier in this chapter, "[T]o the degree that we look at our own works, even if only for assurance, we do, in fact, divide the focus from a Christ alone perspective"?[31] Don't rewards detract from Christ alone? The answer is "no," and here's why. Works that I do that have eternal value are not works done out of my own strength. Rewards work like this:

(1) I receive eternal life (justification, my initial salvation) by faith alone in Christ alone.

(2) As Christ promised, I received the Holy Spirit the instant I believed. One of His roles is to provide the power for me to live a godly life.

(3) Whatever gifts and abilities I have come because God gave them to me (e.g. spiritual gifts, 1 Cor 12:18).

(4) Whatever positive fruit or growth is produced in the believer is the result of God's work in and through him (the fruit of the Spirit [Gal 5:22-23] and the fruit produced by abiding in Christ [John 15:1-6]). In fact, Jesus puts it this way: "I am the vine; you are the branches. Whoever abides in me and I in him, he it is that bears much fruit, for apart from me you can do nothing" (John 15:5). "Nothing" here means the believer produces nothing of eternal value (fruit) without abiding in Him.

(5) The believer's role in this is faithful obedience, with *faithful* as the key word. Paul, after carefully explaining that justification is by faith in Jesus Christ and not by works of the law (Gal 2:16) says, "the life I now live in the flesh I live *by faith* in the Son of God, who loved me and gave himself for me" (Gal 2:20b, emphasis added). Initially, Paul believed the message and was justified; after that initial salvation, he continued to live

---

[30] Dispensational Theology in general and Free Grace theology in particular distinguish the Bema and the Great White Throne. They see these as two different events, at different times, with different participants, with different purposes. The Bema judgment evaluates all believers for faithfulness, and evaluates the quality of their works, which results in reward or loss of reward for the believer. Only unbelievers appear at the Great White Throne Judgment (Rev 20:11-15) at which their unbelief is confirmed and, without exception, each participant is eternally relegated to "the lake of fire." Some outside of Dispensational Theology do not see these two judgments as separate events. For example, Grudem sees them as part of one final judgment. (Grudem, *Systematic Theology*, p. 1141.)

[31] See fn 1 in the present chapter, p. 89.

by faith as He obeyed God. It was an active faith, and Paul's example shows believers of all eras that any works of value the believer does after salvation are produced by living "by faith in the Son of God," not by his or her own initiative or energy.

(6) At the Bema, Jesus then rewards us—for something that fundamentally comes entirely from the Godhead working in and through us to accomplish His purposes. Thus, even rewards, properly understood, exalt Christ. They are a demonstration of His love (by rewarding His people) for faithfully obeying God.

(7) In Rev 4:10-11, which occurs after the rapture of the church and after the Bema evaluation, the twenty-four elders "cast their crowns before the throne," and then worship, saying, "Worthy are you, our Lord and God, to receive glory and honor and power, for you created all things, and by your will they existed and were created." Thus, if this passage is typical of the actions of the raptured church, it demonstrates that Christ is exalted again when our rewards are returned to Christ as an act of worship.

Of course, this key passage on the Bema seat does include a negative dimension to it. Paul doesn't simply assert positive rewards, but he also says people will receive for what they have done that is evil. The word here is *phaulos*, one of eleven words translated *evil* in the ESV. It is also one of the least-used words translated "evil" (only three of the 116 occurrences of *evil*).[32] This version of *evil* has less to do with moral corruption or wickedness and more to do to with worthlessness. One major lexicon defines it as (1) "pert[aining] to being low-grade or morally substandard, *base*," or (2) pert[aining] to being relatively inferior in quality, *ordinary*."[33] Such evil done by the believer would certainly include any moral wickedness he or she committed, but it would also include anything humanly good but done "apart from Him."

Debate exists within Free Grace circles about what these negative consequences might be, whether only the failure to receive positive rewards (thus, fewer crowns received, for example) or actually receiving some sort of negative consequence. Regardless, the Bema exalts Christ when positive

---

[32] Occurring six times in the New Testament, *phaulos* is translated *evil* in John 5:29, 2 Cor 5:10, and Titus 2:8; *wicked* in John 3:20; *bad* in Rom 9:11; and *vile* in Jas 3:6. The two most common words translated *evil* are *ponēros*, sixty-three times, and *kakos*, thirty-two times. Eight other Greek terms are translated *evil*, each three or fewer times.

[33] BDAG, s.v. *phaulos*.

rewards are given that glorify Him. It also exalts Him when negative consequences are given, whatever they may be, because they demonstrate that God holds the believer accountable for following Jesus and confirms that nothing done apart from Him has any eternal value. In both cases, the focus is on the greatness of Christ.

Summary and Conclusion

Every system of theology that promotes some form of "saved by faith alone in Jesus Christ" presents itself as a system that exalts Christ, and, likely, if pressed, adherents of every system would argue *their* system exalts Him more than others. Free Grace genuinely exalts Christ, and, in the opinion of this writer, does so to the greatest degree because it alone places the entire process of salvation, security, assurance, and motivation for service at the feet of Jesus. The individual's sole response is faith, whether faith resulting in initial salvation, or faith as the basis for daily living and serving. Free Grace also exalts Christ in recognizing that He, after giving the believer everything he needs for life and service, chooses to reward him for faithfulness in using what He has provided for His purposes. And it exalts Christ in acknowledging that even the wayward believer is securely held by His hand, despite how that believer is living. Every aspect of our salvation points to the greatness of Christ and His work, to the praise of His glory.

FREE GRACE INTERPRETATIONS HAVE GREAT EXPLANATORY POWER

By Jody Dillow

Not long ago I received a letter from a prisoner who told me he was in prison because of some life changing mistakes he had made and regretted. While there, he read a book I wrote on Free Grace theology,[1] and it apparently had a great impact on his life. In his letter he made this comment, "For the first time in my life, many seemingly contradictory passages of Scripture began to make sense."

Since writing that book, I have received numerous letters from around the world echoing similar sentiments. A woman from Tennessee wrote:

> I finished this book sitting on my front porch at dawn this morning. I cried a long time. It wasn't the first time I had cried while reading it. It is not that the book is depressing, nor should its validity be gauged by how much emotional response it generates. It is that I have been deeply moved, profoundly changed forever by reading it. So many haunting discrepancies in doctrine were cleared up, but the impact is not primarily intellectual.

A new Christian in the Philippines wrote:

> At last, someone has explained some passages in the New Testament which seem to teach that salvation is by works. I knew they could not be teaching that, but on the surface it looked as if they did. Now I think in a different perspective.

These comments are not rare. I have heard them in private conversations at Bible conferences and over many cups of coffee. There is something about the Free Grace interpretations that just seem to make sense

---

[1] Dillow, *The Reign of the Servant Kings.* This can be purchased at www.jodydillow.com.

and resolve numerous interpretive difficulties. For many it provides a dramatic new paradigm regarding the New Testament teachings on salvation, assurance, and rewards.

In my own life, I went through this total paradigm shift a number of years ago. I emerged from the doctoral program in systematic theology with a moderately Reformed view of the theology of the Bible. It made sense (mostly) and gave me a system for understanding the meaning of its teachings. Not only that, it had a wonderful heritage going back to John Calvin, Martin Luther and the magnificent Westminster Confession of 1643. While I was aware of many passages of Scripture that did not seem to fit easily into this system, I assumed in the course of time and with further study, I would get all that sorted out. After a brief stint of teaching at Trinity Evangelical Divinity School (TEDS), in 1978 my wife and I and our three children moved to Vienna, Austria, to begin a covert biblical education by extension ministry behind the Iron Curtain. The beginning of my paradigm shift occurred in Romania.

Romania in the 1980s was not the most desirable place to be. The people were brutally oppressed by one of the most despotic dictators in Eastern Europe, Nicolae Ceaucescu. In this ruthless police state, all the phones were bugged, and many of the people were on the payroll of the Securitate (secret police). Believers were routinely harassed, denied good jobs, interrogated, refused admission to the universities, and sometimes imprisoned because of their stand for Christ.

Yet, in the midst of this Communist control, there was a thriving church of Baptists, Brethren, Pentecostals, Reformed, Lutheran, and Romanian Orthodox. The highlight of my ministry life was working with these wonderful people for fourteen years while we lived in and traveled from Vienna, Austria.[2]

On one of my first trips into this country, I met with a delightful group of Baptist pastors in Bucharest, a twenty-seven hour train ride from Vienna. After leaving the train station, we carefully made our way through the winding streets of the city, alert to avoid being followed by the secret police. Our destination was a humble Baptist church on Popa

---

[2] For many years the Bible delivery ministries (a.k.a "Bible smugglers") had been delivering Bibles across these barbed wire and machine gun guarded borders to thousands of believers hungry to know the Scriptures. In 1979 a historic meeting took place in Vienna in which a number of these missions gathered to explore the possibility of a joint co-operative project to launch a covert extension biblical training program behind the Iron Curtain. God met all of us in an amazing way, and together these missions formed an entity which came to be known as Biblical Education by Extension, or BEE. These missions had concluded that the real need was no longer for more Bibles, but for trained people who could teach the Bible, and thus BEE was born.

Rusu nr. 22. Upon entering the church, we were met with the usual warmth and joy of the Romanian people. The twelve pastors gathered around a table in a room warmed by a coal heated stove, sipped very sweet Romanian coffee and settled in for forty hours of study of Hebrews chapters one to six.

Although I had been teaching the Bible for many years in the United States, I had never met a group so thirsty to know and teach their Bibles. It was a joy to be with them. As we journeyed through the first six chapters of the Epistle to the Hebrews, the teaching was periodically interrupted with shouts of "Fantastic! Fantastic!" They would raise their hands begging me to slow down so they could record every word (that never happened to me in the US!).

Things went well until we came to the sixth chapter of Hebrews. When they discovered that I believed in eternal security, they were astonished. "How," they wondered, "could anyone believe this?" Of course, a central passage for them, was Heb 6:4-6 in which the writer speaks of a saved person who has "fallen away". They were not argumentative, and the discussion that followed was energetic and warm. One of them, Valsile Talosh, who later became a close friend, was a trained lawyer and he led the cross-examination.

Following in the footsteps of their Berean forebears who "received the word with all eagerness, examining the Scriptures daily to see if these things were so, " they asked me to return a few months later so they could study further "to see if these things were so."[3] For several days we went through many passages of the New Testament which seemed to them to show that salvation could be lost. For the most part, they seemed to accept my explanations as plausible.

However, there was a problem. As I walked home each night and prayed and reflected on the conversation of the preceding hours, I realized that I was very inconsistent in how I interpreted many of the relevant scriptures. I had dealt with the warning passages in the book of Hebrews in one way, and the warnings in the rest of the New Testament in another. To explain Hebrews 6, I suggested that this warning was addressed to true believers who were being warned about falling away from the path to maturity and a loss of reward-inheritance (to be discussed below); not loss of salvation. But in the rest of the New Testament when we interacted on John 15, or Col 1:22-23, for example, I said these warnings were addressed to people who had only professed faith in Christ, and they were being warned that

---

[3] Acts 17:11

if they did not make their profession real by reexamining their foundations, repenting, and believing in Christ from the heart, they were in
danger of eternal separation from God. In other words, they were not in
danger of losing salvation because they never had it to begin with.

My approach to understanding the warning passages lacked *coherence*.
That is, I was using one approach in one part of the New Testament, but
had to abandon it in others.

This inconsistency troubled me, and I began to doubt my approach.
It seemed to me that a careful reading of all these warning passages indi-
cated that in fact most of them were addressed to believers, as my Romanian interlocutors insisted, and not to mere professors of faith in Christ.
But there was danger of loss. As I came to realize that in Hebrews I was
answering from one perspective, but in the rest of the New Testament I
was answering from my (formerly) Reformed perspective, I began eight
years of research on this subject which resulted in my book, *The Reign of
the Servant Kings: A Study of Eternal Security and the Final Significance of
Man*. As a result of this research, my mind and spirit were drawn to a new
paradigm for understanding the soteriology of the Bible, a Free Grace
paradigm. What is a paradigm?

Paradigms

Originally a Greek scientific term, the word *paradigm* today more commonly refers to a perception, a model, or a frame of reference. This refers
to the way we *see* the world. Paradigms have considerable influence in
how we interpret the Bible. They affect how we perceive many passages,
and they are lurking in the background of virtually every conclusion we
make. We seldom question their accuracy, and we are often unaware that
we even have them. We commonly *assume* that the way we see things is
the way they really are. Our attitudes, behaviors, and even our theology
often grows out of these assumptions. This is one reason two theologians
can look at the same data and come to radically opposite conclusions. It
is not that the facts are different; instead the paradigms they bring to the
facts strongly influence their interpretations.

The late Stephen Covey illustrates this phenomenon with an experience
that happened to him one Sunday morning on a subway in New York.[4]
People were sitting quietly. Some were reading newspapers, some were
lost in thought, and some were resting, their eyes closed. It was apparently

---

[4] Stephen R. Covey, *The Seven Habits of Highly Effective People* (New York: Schuster, 1989), p. 31.

a calm, peaceful scene. Then suddenly a man and his children entered the subway. The children were so loud and rambunctious that the whole climate changed instantly. People in the subway were distracted and upset.

The father sat down next to him and closed his eyes, apparently oblivious to the situation. The children were yelling and throwing things, even grabbing people's papers. It was quite disturbing. And yet, while all this was going on, the man sitting next to Covey did nothing. It was difficult not to feel irritated. Covey could not believe that this man could be so insensitive as to let his children run wild like that and do nothing about it, taking no responsibility at all. It was easy to see that everyone else on the subway felt irritated too. Finally Covey, with what he felt was unusual patience and restraint, turned to the man and said, "Sir, your children are really disturbing a lot of people. I wonder if you couldn't control them a little more?"

The man lifted his gaze as if to come to a consciousness of the noise for the first time and said softly, "Oh, you're right. I guess I should do something about it. We just came from the hospital where their mother died about an hour ago. I don't know what to think, and I guess they don't know how to handle it either."

Covey continues:

> Can you imagine what I felt at that moment? My paradigm shifted. Suddenly I *saw* things differently, and because I *saw* differently, I *thought* differently, I *felt* differently, I *behaved* differently. My irritation vanished. I didn't have to worry about controlling my attitude or my behavior; my heart was filled with the man's pain. Feelings of sympathy and compassion flowed freely. "Your wife just died? Oh, I'm so sorry! Can you tell me about it? What can I do to help?" Everything changed in an instant.[5]

You have read a number of chapters written by the authors of this book. In order for some readers of this book to share the authors' conclusions, they will need to undergo a paradigm shift. Such a shift often happens after we have reflected on things and sincerely tried to see them from a different point of view. This is that "Aha!" experience we feel when things fall into place for the first time. That happened many times to me as I began to grasp the Free Grace interpretive paradigm.

I concluded that my theological traditions sometimes hindered rather than illuminated my understanding of the Bible. That "Aha!" experience

---

[5] *Ibid.*, pp. 30-31.

occurred over and over as I proceeded on my journey of discovery. Perplexing passages of scripture were coming together to reveal a coherent, consistent understanding of New Testament soteriology. This change was not easy for me. In fact, it took about eight years of biblical study before I was confident enough to make the change. During my study, I identified five pillars of the Free Grace Paradigm.

The Five Pillars of the Free Grace Paradigm

The task of the systematic theologian is to collect all the data of biblical revelation and organize it into a coherent system of thought, a paradigm, which explains the biblical worldview. It was John Calvin who first gave Protestants a model for a systematic theology in his *Institutes of the Christian Religion*. Most Christians are generally aware that in the history of the Church, there have been two major paradigms, or systems of theology, which have predominated: Calvinism and Arminianism. In this book we have presented a third option, a mediating position between the followers of Calvin (the Reformed system)[6] and the followers of Jacob Arminius and John Wesley (the Arminian system).[7] We call it the "Free Grace" paradigm. It has five pillars.

Pillar 1: Salvation comes to us freely through faith alone, but discipleship requires works.

Pillar 2: The are two kinds of inheritance in the Bible.

Pillar 3: There are two dimensions to eternal life.

Pillar 4: It is possible for saved people to fail and become carnal.

Pillar 5: Salvation is by faith alone, but rewards in heaven are obtained by works.

---

[6] Contemporary advocates of the Reformed faith are John Piper, Thomas Schreiner, John McArthur, and R.C Sproul. An excellent systematic theology from this perspective is Berkhof, *Systematic Theology*.

[7] A number of prominent scholars hold the Arminian view: I. Howard Marshall and Gordon Fee. Some recent theological works explaining this paradigm are F. Leroy Forlines, *Classical Arminianism: A Theology of Salvation* (Randall House Publications, 2011). and Robert E. Picirilli, *Grace, Faith, Free Will* (Randall House Publications, 2002).

Pillar 1: Salvation Comes to Us Freely through Faith Alone, but Discipleship Requires Works.

Fundamental to the Free Grace paradigm is the fact the New Testament affirms that salvation comes to us through faith alone and works have no part. Scripture is plain:

> For if Abraham was justified by works, he has something to boast about, but not before God. For what does the Scripture say? "ABRAHAM BELIEVED GOD, AND IT WAS CREDITED TO HIM AS RIGHTEOUSNESS." Now to the one who works, his wage is not credited as a favor, but as what is due. But to the one who does not work, but believes in Him who justifies the ungodly, his faith is credited as righteousness, (Rom 4:2-5, NASB95)

> He saved us, *not on the basis of deeds which we have done in righteousness*, but according to His mercy, by the washing of regeneration and renewing by the Holy Spirit, (Titus 3:5, NASB95, emphasis added.)

> Then He said to me, "It is done. I am the Alpha and the Omega, the beginning and the end. I will give to the one who thirsts from the spring of *the water of life without cost*." (Revelation 21:6, NASB95, emphasis added)

While all Protestants agree with this, how they handle the passages which seem to teach otherwise differs dramatically. Much of the disagreement is related to how interpreters understand the meaning of *save* in many of the relevant passages.

After leaving graduate school, I, of course, knew that the verb *to save* (Gr *sōzō*) and the noun *salvation* (Gr *sōtēria*) do not necessarily always refer to deliverance from final damnation. For example, in Matt 9:22, Jesus says to the woman with a hemorrhage who touched his robe, "your faith has healed you [Gr *sōzō*]." Here the verb *to save* means "to heal." Also, as Peter was walking on the water toward Jesus and began to sink, he cried, "Lord, save me" (Matt 14:30). Clearly save in that context meant to save him from drowning, not save him from eternal separation from God! Armed with these facts, my mind was open to consider the meaning in a particular context rather than read a particular meaning into most of them. For example, consider the passage that has perplexed interpreters for centuries and caused Luther to proclaim that the epistle of James was an epistle of straw.[8]

> "What use is it, my brethren, if someone says he has faith but he has no works? Can that faith save him?" (Jas 2:14, NASB95)

> "Even so faith, if it has no works, is dead, being by itself." (Jas 2:17, NASB95)

Luther understood *save* to mean "save from damnation" and concluded that James was teaching that works were a condition of salvation in contradiction to Paul. Therefore, he rejected the epistle as part of the canon. Because there is some resistance to the idea that salvation can refer to anything else other than deliverance from post-mortem condemnation to the lake of fire, many Protestant interpreters came to the rescue and said that the text means that a faith which does not result in a life of works is not genuine, that is, it does not save from damnation.

Free Grace interpreters do not believe that *save* in Jas 2:14 refers to this. But to suggest that *save* in James could mean deliverance from something besides damnation is often strongly rejected. For example, one commentator writes, "The lengths to which advocates of this view [i.e., Free Grace] will go to preserve their theology are remarkable," and asserts that to take *save* to refer to a deliverance from physical death "is an astonishing move since salvation and justification are typically associated in the New Testament with entering heaven."[9]

However, there is nothing "remarkable" or "astonishing" about this at all. When James asked, "Can that faith save him?" meaning, it cannot, we must ask two questions, "What is *that* faith?" and "Salvation from what?"

In the New Testament the verb *sōzō* occurs 106 times and the noun *sōtēria* 46 times. The meaning of *sōzō* as "deliver from eternal damnation" is nonexistent in the Old Testament and occurs only forty percent of the time in the New,[10] while *sōtēria* means deliverance from hell only thirty-five percent of the time.[11] The basic idea behind *to save* is

---

[8] Martin Luther, "Preface to the New Testament," in *Word and Sacrament*, ed. Theodor Bachman (Philadelphia: Fortress Press, 1960), 35:362.

[9] Thomas R. Schreiner, "Perseverance and Assurance," *Southern Baptist Journal of Theology* 2, no. 1 (Spring 1998): 45. Schreiner appeals to Jesus' encounter with the rich young ruler to support his thesis that salvation always means deliverance from final damnation.

[10] E.g., Acts 4:12; 11:14; Rom 8:24; 9:27; 1 Cor 5:5; Jude 23.

[11] Acts 4:12; 13:26; Rom 1:16; 10:1; 2 Cor 6:2; Eph 1:13. For discussion, see Joseph C. Dillow, *Final Destiny: The Future Reign of the Servant Kings*, 2nd revised ed. (Monument, CO: Paniym Group, Inc., 2014, 2016), Chapter 28.

to deliver from some difficulty, and the context determines the kind of difficulty in view.[12]

Free Grace interpreters, aware that *save* does not necessarily mean save from damnation and *faith* does not necessarily refer to the initial faith by which a person is saved and justified, wonder what *faith* and *save* mean elsewhere in the book of James.

The word *save* is used five times in James,[13] and, unless 2:14 is an exception, in none of the usages does it refer to salvation from eternal damnation.

In regard to *faith*, all interpreters know that it can mean either the act of initial trust in the person of Christ through which we are justified, or it can mean a walk of faith (e.g. Hebrews 11, etc.).[14] It is used 15 times in James and in every instance it refers to a believer's walk of faith, trusting Christ in daily life, and not initial saving faith.[15] For example, in Jas 1:2-4, it is used of a faith related to testing and enduring trials; initial faith is not in view. Or, consider 2:1 where James speaks of holding one's faith in Christ with an attitude of impartiality. Obviously, the continuing exercise of faith, "holding" it, is in view and not initial inception. James also speaks of the poor who are "rich in faith and heirs

---

[12] See any Greek lexicon. For example, BDAG, gives a number of possible translations depending on the context: "to preserve or rescue from natural dangers and afflictions," "to save, keep from harm, preserve, rescue," "save from death," or "save/free from disease," p. 982.

[13] James 1:21; 2:14; 4:12; 5:11; 5:20. In 4:12 it refers to divine discipline on the believer in time; in 5:11, it refers to physical healing; and in 5:20 *save* refers to salvation from the sin which can lead to the judgment of physical death. Regarding Jas 1:21, in which he speaks of the implanted word being able to "save your souls," it should be noted that this phrase and related ones occur fourteen times in the Old Testament and they never mean "save from hell." In each instance it refers to the salvation of one's physical life or rescue from some temporal trial. This phrase or similar ones are found fourteen times in the LXX (Gen 19:17, 20; 32:30; Judg 12:3; Job 33:28; Pss 3:3; 6:5; 34:3; 42:11; 68:2; 73:13; 85:2; Amos 2:14, 16). In each case, the phrase suggests the notion of preserving one's physical life. In Gen 19:17, the LXX translates, "save your soul;" and in Gen 32:30, Jacob, after his struggle with the Angel of the Lord, exclaims, "My life (LXX Gr *psyche*, "soul," Heb *nepeš*) has been preserved (i.e., "saved," Gr *sōzō*, Heb *nāsal*)." In one passage it refers to delivering the needy from social injustice (Ps 72:13) by preserving their lives. Even the warrior, declares Amos, will "not save his life" in the coming invasion (Amos 2:14, 16). In Ps 42:11 (LXX, 41:12), David's soul ("life" Gr *psychē*), is in despair so he turns to God for "help of my countenance," which in the LXX is "salvation (Gr *sōtēria*) of my countenance." In 1 Sam 19:5, 1 Kgs 19:5 LXX), David took his life (Gr *psychē*) in his hand and killed Goliath, and this resulted in salvation (Gr *sōtēria*) of all Israel, including, of course, David. Salvation from enemies is the meaning. Similarly, in Ps 3:2, David once again finds many enemies saying that God will not save (LXX Gr *sōzō*) him. In Ps 35:3, he asks the Lord to save his soul (LXX Gr *psychē*), and God responds, "I am your salvation (Gr *sōtēria*)." He wants deliverance from those who are his enemies and who fight against him (v 2).

[14] *Faith*, viewed as a walk of faith and not the faith that initially justified, is found in many places in the New Testament. See Rom 14:23; 2 Cor 5:7; 10:15; Gal 3:11; 5:6; 1 Tim 1:4-5; 6:12; etc.

[15] For example, see Jas 1:3, 6; 2:1, 5, 14 (2x), 17, 18 (3x), 20, 22, 24, 26; 5:15.

of the kingdom" (2:5). To be "rich in faith" is not a reference to the initial act of faith that procures salvation from damnation; instead, it refers to being "rich in the sphere of faith."[16]

Based upon James's usage, one can conclude that James is not talking about a saving faith that is "dead," instead, he refers to a walk of faith that is not energized by works and is therefore not vital or useful, that is, it is "dead" (2:17). It is unable to save in the sense of salvation from spiritual and psychological ruin (i.e., "death" in 1:21)[17] and from a negative assessment on one's life at the Judgment Seat of Christ (2:12-13).[18] James is speaking about discipleship, not initial salvation.

The Free Grace approach to interpretation does not read ideas into James that are foreign to what he is saying. It is coherent; it has explanatory power. It easily resolves a difficulty that troubled Luther and a host of interpreters ever since. One can take Scripture at face value.

The distinction between salvation by faith and discipleship by works must be maintained if we are to have any hope of understanding numerous passages in the New Testament. The problem is particularly acute in the Gospels in which, in many passages, Jesus seems to be teaching that works are in some way necessary for salvation, either on the front end by submission to Christ's lordship, or on the back end by a life of holiness to the final hour. In fact, many liberal theologians have concluded that the theology of Paul and that of Jesus are simply irreconcilable and that Paul did not derive his views from Christ.[19]

For example, based on many of the passages we have quoted above and particularly passages in Matthew and Luke, Catholics have argued that works are clearly conditions for entering the kingdom of heaven. Calvin had a ready reply: works are not a *condition* of entrance; they describe the *character* of all who will, i.e., "the faith that saves is not alone." This solution is widespread. Based upon Matt 5:28-29, John Piper told his

---

[16] Martin Dibelius and Heinrich Greeven, *James: A Commentary on the Epistle of James*, 11th rev. ed., Hermeneia (Philadelphia: Fortress Press, 1975), p. 124.

[17] See Dillow, *Final Destiny*, pp. 397-402.

[18] *Ibid.*, pp. 402-407. The immediate context of 2:14 does not refer to the eternal damnation (v 13); instead it is speaking of a judgment on the believer's works or lack of them at the Judgment Seat of Christ. Eternal damnation is not even mentioned.

[19] For the classical refutation of this liberal perspective, see J. Gresham Machen, *The Origin of St. Paul's Religion* (n.p.: Amazon Digital Services, 1921, 2014). Also, J. Gresham Machen, *Christianity and Liberalism*, new ed. (Grand Rapids: Wm. B. Eerdmans Publishing Company, 1946). For a recent discussion of this issue, see Roger Mohrlang, *Matthew and Paul: A Comparison of Ethical Perspectives*, Monograph series / Society for New Testament Studies (New York: Cambridge University Press, 1984).

congregation "If you are not struggling against lust, you are going to hell."[20] Jesus also said, that if we have ever been angry or called someone a fool, that we "shall be guilty *enough to go* into the fiery hell" (5:21-22).

Those who reject the Free Grace Paradigm sometimes get themselves twisted up like a pretzel in their attempts to explain all the passages which seem to say works are a condition, a demonstration, or a cause of salvation. When in fact, most of the passages they cite are not calls to salvation, but rather to fully committed discipleship. For example, Alan Stanley, who is a godly, gracious, and scholarly missionary, has recently published a book entitled *Salvation Is More Complicated Than You Think*. Because he rejects the Free Grace paradigm and the distinction between salvation and discipleship, Dr. Stanley's explanation of many works passages in Matthew does indeed appear like something purchased at Auntie Ann's pretzel stand.

On the one hand, Stanley says he agrees with Luther that "works are not the cause of one's salvation but the result,"[21] but, on the other hand, Stanley says he agrees with Calvin that works are an "inferior cause."[22] On the one hand, he states "that the salvation yet to be attained in eternity is secure right now though not complete." But on the other hand, he says, "There are also passages…that teach the possibility of forfeiting salvation through lack of endurance."[23] On the one hand, he tells us that endurance

---

[20] John Piper, "Battling the Unbelief of Lust," Nov 13th, 1988. Audio and text available online at http://www.desiringgod.org/messages/battling-the-unbelief-of-lust. Last accessed Oct 21st, 2016.

[21] Stanley, *Did Jesus Teach Salvation by Works?* p. 321. Stanley would probably say that Luther is speaking of pre-conversion works, leaving open whether post-conversion works save. However, Luther would maintain that no works of any kind, pre or post-conversion, can save. Stanley quotes Luther as saying, "For we perceive that a man who is justified is not yet a righteous man, but is in the very movement or journey toward righteousness." Martin Luther, *The Disputation Concerning Justification*, ed. J. J. Pelikan, H. C. Oswald, and H. T. Lehman, Luther's Works (Philadelphia: Fortress Press, 1999), p. 23. However, what Luther meant by "journey toward righteousness" is not, as Stanley implies, a journey toward final salvation from eternal damnation; rather it is the journey of progressive sanctification, becoming righteous in experience just as we are by forensic imputation. Here is what Luther actually said: "23. For we perceive that a man who is justified is not yet a righteous man, but is in the very movement or journey toward righteousness. 24. Therefore, whoever is justified is still a sinner; and yet he is considered fully and perfectly righteous by God who pardons and is merciful. 25. Moreover, God forgives and is merciful to us because Christ, our advocate and priest, intercedes and sanctifies our beginning in righteousness. 26. His righteousness, since it is without defect and serves us like an umbrella against the heat of God's wrath, does not allow our beginning righteousness to be condemned." *Ibid.*, pp. 23-26. One possesses a full and perfect righteousness when he believes, but he must make it experiential.

[22] Stanley, *Did Jesus Teach Salvation by Works?* p. 322. See below where it will be argued that this was not Calvin's view.

[23] *Ibid.*, p. 327.

is a "condition because salvation hasn't occurred yet." On the other hand, he says, "It is quite incorrect to say that endurance is an addition to the gospel."[24] On the one hand, he says that "endurance [i.e., post-conversion, God-produced, non-meritorious, work] does not, in agreement with the Reformers' viewpoint, cause [final] salvation,"[25] but is only a "constituent part" or "intrinsic aspect" of it.[26] On the other hand, he agrees with Calvin's supposed view that works are a "minor" cause.[27] On the one hand, he insists that entering the kingdom is by faith alone, but, on the other hand, he says, "Somewhere along the way converted sinners evidently become righteous and therefore eligible to enter the kingdom."[28] On the one hand, he maintains that there is a distinction between a condition and a cause[29] and that salvation is not "caused" by works, while, on the other hand, he states that final salvation is a "consequence" of works,[30] is "based" on works,[31] and has works as a "minor cause," thereby seemingly closely relating the ideas of condition and cause. He says works are a condition for (final) salvation but not a demonstration of it because final salvation has not occurred yet, but he goes on to say that works are a condition of final salvation in the sense that they are a demonstration of initial salvation. One gets lost in all these fine distinctions and wonders how a fisherman in the first century would ever have understood Jesus. Drawing

---

[24] *Ibid.*, pp. 252-53.

[25] *Ibid.*, p. 320.

[26] *Ibid.*, p. 252. Notice all the qualifiers one must insert to make Stanley's views clear. How would any reader of the New Testament pick up on all these subtleties?

[27] *Ibid.*, pp. 51, 322. Admittedly, Calvin spoke rather opaquely. John Calvin, "Prefatory Address to Francis, King of France," in *Institutes of the Christian Religion* (Grand Rapids: Wm. B. Eerdmans Publishing Co., 1964), 3.14.6. But it is not clear that Calvin is defining *cause* the same way Stanley defines it. Calvin asserts, "What precedes in the order of administration is called the cause of what follows." It is not really a cause but is only called that because works precede entrance into heaven. Calvin explicitly clarified what he meant when he said, "There are inferior causes, but these depend on free justification, which is the only true cause of why God blesses us. These modes of expression designate the order of sequence rather than the cause." For Stanley, *cause* means "something which brings about an effect," but it is likely that Calvin simply means "something which precedes something else in a sequence."

[28] Stanley, *Did Jesus Teach Salvation by Works?* p. 175.

[29] Stanley asserts that works are a "condition" of salvation, but then he begins to qualify that statement: "It is unfortunate that the term 'condition' carries with it all sorts of negative connotations, for Jesus does not mean condition here in the sense of gaining merit or favor." He then says that by condition he means that "one must continue in their already existing relationship with God if they are to be finally saved." *Ibid.*, p. 248.

[30] Calvin, quoted in *Ibid.*, p. 322.

[31] Stanley says, "People will be judged on the basis of their works vis-à-vis their eternal destiny." *Ibid.*, p. 311.

a line between a "condition," a "consequence," a "basis,"[32] a "cause," a "constituent part" or an "intrinsic aspect" would appear to many to be distinctions without significant differences. Stanley admits that some of these contrasts seem to be contradictory and there is a "tension" here. One is reminded of the man who throws ash up in the air, and as it cascades around him complains, "I cannot see."[33]

Imagine the following dialogue as an advocate of Stanley's views (as set forth in his book, *Salvation Is More Complicated Than You Think*), shares the gospel with an unbeliever, whom we will call Bill.

> Counselor: Bill, I would like to share with you the wonderful good news of God's free offer of eternal life that comes without cost.
>
> Bill: How can I obtain this free gift without cost? Please explain the gospel to me. How can I become a Christian?
>
> Counselor: You must believe on the Lord Jesus Christ, and if your believing is sincere, you will be saved.
>
> Bill: How will I know if I am sincere enough?
>
> Counselor: You will progress to a point at which you possess surpassing righteousness, and then you will be eligible to enter the kingdom.
>
> Bill: What does that involve?
>
> Counselor: Well, you will need to obey all the commands,[34] sell your wealth and give it to the poor,[35] always forgive others,[36]

---

[32] Stanley says that the eschatological judgment (entrance into heaven) is "based on works." *Ibid.*, p. 133.

[33] Stanley might explain these seeming discrepancies this way: "If a person is truly saved, he will have post-conversion works. These works must be there from beginning to end of the salvation process before a person can enter heaven. But during the process the same works are viewed from two different perspectives, depending on which way a person is viewing salvation: (1) looking back on initial salvation, these works are a demonstration of faith, because salvation has been attained; (2) looking forward to final salvation, these works are a condition of salvation because that final salvation hasn't been attained yet. In other words, works are at the same time a demonstration and a condition, depending on the perspective. Demonstration points to successful accomplishment; condition points to potential accomplishment. In either case, the works have to be there before a person can claim to be saved. Conditional works are a demonstration of works waiting to happen." (Suggested by Wendall Hollis, personal communication, April 7, 2008).

[34] Matt 5:20; 7:21; John 15:14; Jas 2:17

[35] Matt 19:21

[36] Matt 6:14-15

be a peacemaker,[37] completely deny yourself to the point of possible martyrdom,[38] obey everything the Bible teaches, develop a personal character that surpasses the highest known standards of character in Jesus' day,[39] always struggle against lust,[40] never develop anger as a pattern of life,[41] do acts of kindness toward others,[42] strive to be perfect,[43] abandon everything to follow Christ,[44] and a few other things.

Bill: Do I have to make a commitment to do all these things in order for my faith to be genuine?

Counselor: That seems to be what Jesus is teaching. You must commit to live out the principles of the Sermon on the Mount.

Bill: I thought you said salvation is by faith alone, is a gift, and is offered to me without cost.

Counselor: Well, Bill… salvation is more complicated than you think.

If Dr. Stanley could clearly distinguish between the biblical teaching that salvation is by faith alone and the passages he cites in Matthew, which are calls to discipleship and not initial salvation, he would find that the problem of works salvation in Matthew would evaporate. Soteriology is not Matthew's main concern, rather he is addressing those who are already Christians and setting forth Jesus' demands to live like Christians.

Pillar 2: The Are Two Kinds of Inheritance in the Bible

As I attempted to resolve the tension created in part by my Romanian interlocutors, the concept of the believer's inheritance cropped up many times in my thinking. What perplexed me was that while it was obvious that in many passages our inheritance was "heaven when we die" and comes to us by faith alone and for no other reason (e.g. Gal 3:29), in other places it was a reward obtained by works (e.g. Col 3:24). In

---

[37] Matt 5:9

[38] Matt 16:24-25

[39] Matt 5:20

[40] Matt 5:27-29

[41] Matt 5:21-22

[42] Matt 25:34-40

[43] Matt 5:48

[44] Matt 8:19-22

other words, there seems to be a dual inheritance: one based on faith alone (salvation-inheritance), and another based on works of perseverance (reward-inheritance).[45] That idea was completely new to me. If it was true, it would resolve a problem in many passages which seem to teach that arrival in heaven is conditioned not on faith alone, but also on works—*if* the inheritance always refers to heaven. The passages which promise the inheritance as a reward to works do not refer to heaven but to our reward there, a reward-inheritance. On the other hand, the passages which promised the inheritance to faith alone refer to our final entrance into the presence of Christ, that is, our salvation-inheritance.

For example, the Rich Young Ruler asked Jesus, "Good Teacher, what shall I do to inherit eternal life?" (Mark 10:17) Surely if Jesus understood him to be asking about final entrance into heaven, He would have said to the young man what He said to Nicodemus, "whoever believes in Him should not perish, but have eternal life." Instead, He says, "You know the commandments…" telling him to obey the Law. Jesus is referring to the "reward-inheritance."

There are many passages easily explained if we understand them as references to the reward-inheritance.[46] There are passages which clearly teach a dual inheritance.[47] For example, "knowing that from the Lord you will receive the reward [Gr *antapodosis*] of the inheritance. It is the Lord Christ whom you serve" (Col 3:24, NASB95).

Colossians 3:24 is particularly interesting. In that passage Paul speaks of the inheritance as a reward. The Greek word, *antapodosis*, refers to a

---

[45] For those who would like to verify this for themselves, I have listed all instances of the noun and verbal forms of "inherit." The verb *to inherit* (Gr *klēronomeō*) is found eighteen times in the New Testament: Matt 5:5; 19:29; 25:34; Mark 10:17; Luke 10:25; 18:18; 1 Cor 6:9, 10; 15:50; Gal 4:30; 5:21; Heb 1:4, 14; 6:12; 1 Pet 3:9; Rev 21:7. The noun *heir* (Gr *klēronomos*, "heir, beneficiary" BDAG, p. 548) occurs in fifteen passages: Matt 21:38; Mark 12:7; Luke 20:14; Rom 4:13, 14; 8:17; Gal 3:29; 4:1, 7; Titus 3:7; Heb 1:2; 6:17; 11:7; Jas 2:5. The related noun, *inheritance* (Gr *klēronomia*) occurs fourteen times: Matt 21:38; Mark 12:7; Luke 12:13; 20:14; Acts 7:5; 20:32; Gal 3:18; Eph 1:14, 18; 5:5; Col 3:24; Heb 9:15; 11:8; 1 Pet 1:4.

[46] For example, "And everyone who has left houses or brothers or sisters or father or mother or children or farms for My name's sake, will receive many times as much, and will inherit eternal life" (Matt 19:29, NASB95). Is this a requirement for salvation without cost and by faith alone? "[N]or thieves, nor the covetous, nor drunkards, nor revilers, nor swindlers, will inherit the kingdom of God" (1 Cor 6:10, NASB95). Is it impossible for bad people, like Solomon or Saul, to go to heaven? "[E]nvying, drunkenness, carousing, and things like these, of which I forewarn you, just as I have forewarned you, that those who practice such things will not inherit the kingdom of God" (Gal 5:21, NASB95).

[47] Romans 8:17 speaks of being "heirs of God," and also being co-heirs of Christ if we persevere in suffering. For discussion see, Dillow, *Final Destiny*, pp. 83-88.

"recompense, reward for what has been done."[48] Jesus uses this word for reward in Luke 14:14: "and you will be blessed, since they do not have the means to repay you; for you will be repaid [Gr *antapodosis*] at the resurrection of the righteous." (Luke 14:14, NASB95). Since we know that heaven is not payment for work done and is ours by faith alone, Jesus must refer to the reward-inheritance.

If one acknowledges this biblically derived conclusion, as Free Grace interpreters do, a myriad of perplexing passages regarding works and salvation are clarified. For example, consider Heb 11:7:

> By faith Noah, being warned by God about things not yet seen, in reverence prepared an ark for the salvation of his household, by which he condemned the world, and became an heir of the righteousness which is according to faith. (NASB95)

Because many interpreters assume that "the righteousness which is according to faith" refers to justifying righteousness, an obvious problem arises. On that assumption, Noah was saved by his life of faithful obedience to Yahweh in preparing the ark. But, we ask, "How did Noah obtain this verdict of righteousness?" He obtained it because he "in reverence prepared an ark for the salvation of his household, by which he condemned the world." He obtained it by works. Noah was already a believer before he built this ark. Before he even struck the first nail, God said of him, "But Noah found favor in the eyes of the LORD" (Gen 6:8). He displayed his saved status when he worshiped God "in reverence" as he hammered every nail. Thus, this verdict of righteousness was something added to a salvation which he already possessed.

What does it mean that Noah became "an heir of the righteousness which is according to faith" (Heb 11:7)? What is this "faith" and this "righteousness"? Paul Tanner argues that in Hebrews 11, *faith* does not refer to the initial transaction through which we are born again; rather, *faith* in this chapter refers to the *walk of faith* in every instance.[49] He further points out that the word *righteousness* is used six times in Hebrews and never of imputed righteousness. In each instance it refers to the moral quality of righteousness.[50] Tanner concludes:

> Since "faith" in Hebrews 10-11 is not "saving faith," and since "righteousness" in Hebrews is not "forensic imputed righteousness," this verse is probably talking about something else. Noah

---

[48] Louw and Nida, *Greek-English Lexicon of the New Testament*, s.v. *antapodosis*.

[49] Paul Tanner, personal communication, May 27, 2012.

[50] See Heb 1:9; 5:13; 7:2; 11:33 and 12:11.

was a man of faith, and as Genesis 6:8 teaches us, he was a "righteous and blameless man." So what did that gain him? It qualified (or led to) him becoming an "heir."[51]

Thus, when the writer says Noah inherited the righteousness which is according to faith, we paraphrase, "Noah inherited the moral righteousness corresponding to [his] faithfulness," that is, he became a possessor of a lifestyle which God commended because he lived by faith. He received the reward-inheritance.

The writer of the anonymous homily to the Hebrews tells us that the inheritance comes to us not by faith alone, but by "faith and patience" (Heb 6:12) and John echoes a similar theme teaching us that only "He who overcomes," that is, those who faithfully endure suffering, will "inherit these things" (Rev 21:7, NASB95).

I used to explain these inheritance passages in three ways.

(1) One option suggests that since all true believers have good works to the end of life, these passages about our inheritance being based upon works are not saying the works are a condition of entrance in to heaven, but are characteristic of all who will enter.

(2) Or, perhaps, these passages are implied warnings to those who have professed faith in Christ to remind them that if they do not work, they are not really born again.

(3) A final possibility I considered was that for those who are born again, these passages may be the means God uses to secure their perseverance in good works. He threatens them with the possibility they are not saved. However, while this view is common, it is totally implausible. It teaches that even though God knows they are believers and will go to heaven, He lies to them in order to motivate them. John Calvin actually endorsed this kind of thinking in his discussion of Romans 11 when he said that even though "this cannot happen to the elect [i.e., loss of salvation], they have need of such warning, in order to subdue the pride of the flesh which needs to be terrified with the dread of perdition."[52]

These ad hoc explanations never satisfied me. They were theological ideas imposed upon the text that would never occur to a first century

[51] Paul Tanner, personal communication, May 27, 2012.

[52] John Calvin, *Romans*, Calvin's Commentaries (Albany, OR: Ages Software, 1998), s.v. "Rom. 11:22".

fisherman unfamiliar with post-Reformation polemics. The beauty of the Free Grace Paradigm is that we can make one simple assumption based upon numerous passages: that there are two kinds of inheritance. One kind of inheritance is for reward and is based upon works and the other kind is our final entrance into heaven and comes through faith alone.

Pillar 3: There Are Two Dimensions to Eternal Life

During my last years in the university, I worked for six months in a lumber mill in Springfield, Oregon. We made the laminated beams seen in the ceilings of buildings. One of my jobs was to run the glue machine that glued the beams together. It was an outstanding learning experience for me, because I had never really learned the meaning of work. I arrived in college anticipating a four-year keg-party and did not became a believer until my junior year. Even though I was now a Christ follower, I had a lot to learn about life.

Every day at 4:00, I headed to the lumber mill to glue laminated beams together until midnight. The foreman at this plant had recently become a member of a well-known non-Christian cult (Mormonism), and he was quite excited about his faith. He was a fine man and really helped me learn how to work.

Needless to say, I was anxious to convert him to biblical Christianity, and one night, while on a 30-minute break, I waded in. As I enthusiastically spoke to him of the wonders of salvation by faith alone in Christ alone and apart from works, he pulled out his Bible and read a passage in Romans 2 which says that God,

> WILL RENDER TO EVERY MAN ACCORDING TO HIS DEEDS: to those who by perseverance in doing good seek for glory and honor and immortality, eternal life. (Rom 2:6-7, NASB95)

My boss looked at me and said, "Jody, my Bible says you are wrong."

There it was. Not knowing what to say, I stared blankly at Paul's statement. In the clearest possible words, Paul declares that eternal life is awarded for "doing good" works, not because of faith alone. It is obtained by "perseverance in doing good." Since everyone "knows" that "eternal life" refers to heaven when one dies, it appeared that my Mormon friend had a good argument. Does the Bible teach that salvation is by works?

While in seminary I heard an explanation which seemed like a stretch. I was told that "perseverance in doing good" was not a condition of obtaining eternal life, but was the characteristic of all those who will. So, the verse became a kind of test which believers could apply to determine their saved status. I was always suspicious that this would be the answer because the text seemed clearly to say that it was a condition, not just a characteristic. How else could Paul say it?

Free Grace hermeneutics leads us naturally in a different direction. It forces one to get out a concordance and reflect on the meaning of the phrase *eternal life*. When I did that, an immediate answer was forthcoming which did not involve reading a theological bias into the text. This is why I love the Free Grace approach. My concordance study led me to two well established conclusions.

First, the phrase *eternal life* (Gr *zōē aiōnios*) occurs forty-three times in forty-one verses in the Greek New Testament. Its common meaning of the free gift of regeneration resulting in final entrance into heaven on the basis of faith alone is well documented.

Secondly, every time eternal life is presented as an acquisition in the *future* (fifteen times, or 35%), *it is always based on works*.[53] Eternal life often refers to an enhanced experience of life now (i.e., following conversion) or in the future with God. In the latter case, not just entrance into the kingdom is in view, but an enhanced, abundant entrance rewarded to those who by perseverance in doing good seek for glory and honor (cf. 2 Pet 1:11). To seek honor is to live to hear the Master say, "Well done!" (Matt 25:23). That is the probable meaning of Rom 2:7. Eternal life can not only be richly experienced now, but it can by inherited as a reward for a faithful life (Matt 19:29).

Pillar 4: It Is Possible for Saved People to Fail and Become Carnal

Carnal Christian? Is there such a thing? Or, do all Christians live faithfully, at least for the most part, to the end of life?

I became a Christian at the beginning of my junior year in electrical engineering at Oregon State University. My future wife, Linda, who had become a Christian through Campus Crusade for Christ (now called Cru) a few months earlier immediately got me connected with the Campus Crusade movement at Oregon State University. They followed me up, answered many questions, and ultimately challenged me to go to Dallas

---

[53] Matt 19:16, 29; 25:46 (cf. v. 35); Mark 10:17, 30; Luke 10:25, 30; John 4:36; 6:27; 12:25; Rom 2:7; 6:22; Gal 6:8; Jude 21.

Seminary and then on to missions. Linda and I were on Campus Crusade staff for eight wonderful years.

During that time, and later in seminary, I learned, based upon 1 Cor 3:1-3, that there were three kinds of Christians: baby Christians, mature Christians, and carnal Christians. I was soon to learn that this was a view rejected by some Bible scholars. While the Westminster Confession said a person could be carnal "for a time," if he was truly born again, he would always eventually repent.[54] A life of works inevitably flowed from true, saving faith. Faith without works was *dead*, that is, not genuine faith. As Calvin famously put it, "It is therefore faith alone which justifies, and yet the faith which justifies is not alone."[55] This was a powerful riposte to the Catholic Counter-Reformation at the Council of Trent which accused the Reformers of teaching that works were optional. Furthermore, it was a convenient explanation to the many passages which seemed to teach that faith plus works were necessary for final entrance into heaven.

The problem with this approach is (1) that it is a theological bias not even alluded to in the contexts and is imposed upon these texts; and (2) that it is flatly contradicted by numerous passages of Scripture. In many places the Bible records final failure in the life of people who were genuinely born again.

For example, consider Solomon. All admit that he was a saved person, yet Scripture tells us that he finished life immorally married to foreign women, and he worshiped foreign pagan gods. Sometimes it is argued that when Solomon became old, he repented and wrote the book of Ecclesiastes. However, the writer of First Kings plainly tells us, "For *when Solomon was old*, his wives turned *his heart away after other gods*; and his heart was not wholly devoted to the LORD his God, as the heart of David his father had been." (1 Kgs 11:4, NASB95, emphasis added).

Or consider the life of King Saul, who was clearly a saved man.[56] He had been changed by the Holy Spirit "into another man" (1 Sam 10:6).

---

[54] *Westminster Confession of Faith*, XVII, 3.

[55] John Calvin, *Acts of the Council of Trent: with the Antidote*, 6th Session, can. 11 in H. Beveridge & J. Bonnet, eds. Selected Works of John Calvin (Grand Rapids: Baker, 1983) 3:152.

[56] He was anointed by the Lord as ruler over God's inheritance (1 Sam 10:1, 24), the Spirit of the Lord had come on him "mightily," and he prophesied and had been "changed into another man" by means of the Spirit (vv 6-11). The Spirit of the Lord came on him on one occasion, provoking him to righteous anger (1 Sam 11:6). He expelled all the mediums and spiritualists from the land (1 Sam 28:3). Even in his carnality he remembered that God had answered his prayers in the past (1 Sam 28:15), and he had some faith and inclination to goodness (1 Sam 24:16-21). He still prayed (1 Sam 28:6), and he could still repent. All these things would, of course, indicate to most that Saul was regenerate (1 Sam 26:21, 25).

Yet he became disobedient and forfeited his rulership over the kingdom (1 Sam 13:13-14). He was a deceiver (1 Sam 18:19-29), he murdered the priests of the Lord (1 Sam 22:17-18) and the chronicler summaries his life saying, "Saul died because he was unfaithful to the LORD; he did not keep the word of the LORD and even consulted a medium for guidance, and did not inquire of the LORD. So the LORD put him to death and turned the kingdom over to David son of Jesse" (1 Chr 10:13-14, NIV).

There are many other illustrations of final failure and carnality in the lives of men who were obviously saved. I remember one year in my Bible reading I made it a point to record them all.[57] That said, most Free Grace interpreters do believe that all who have believed will definitely manifest some degree of good works and inner changes of attitude. However, as the above discussion shows, it is possible that some might fall away and finish life walking as a carnal man, or as Paul put it, "walking like mere men" (1 Cor 3:3, NASB95). These people will have no good works or rewards that survive into heaven. All will be burned up, and they will be saved, "yet so as through fire" (1 Cor 3:15).

On one occasion, a good friend and co-worker who strongly denied that the Bible teaches the existence of the carnal Christian challenged me, saying:

> "Jody, can you show me even one verse that proves that a born again believer will not persevere in a life of good works until the final hour."

I said, "Sure," and turned him to the following words from Christ,

> "Whoever then annuls one of the least of these command-ments, and teaches others to do the same, shall be called least *in* the kingdom of heaven; but whoever keeps and teaches them, he shall be called great *in* the kingdom of heaven." (Matt 5:19, NASB95, emphasis added)

Jesus had been accused of abolishing the Law. To the contrary, He says that even the least important laws must be obeyed. He says that the

---

[57] There are many passages which could be cited; the following are representative. While some will argue that a few of these passages are controversial, and that all those who fell away were not saved to begin with, I have demonstrated elsewhere that all of these "failures" were in fact truly born again. For full discussion see Dillow, *Final Destiny*, Chapters 32-33. See Lot (Gen 19:8, 33); Num 16:30-32; Jehu (2 Kgs 10:31); 1 Chr 10:13-24; Rehoboam (2 Chr 12:1-4); Asa (2 Chr 16:7); Joash (2 Chr 24:20); Amaziah (2 Chr 25:2).; Uzziah (2 Chr 26:16); Ezek 18:24; Matt 5:13, 19; 25:1-13; Luke 8:11-15; John 2:23; 6:60-66; 12:42; 13:8-10; Acts 8:20-24; 1 Cor 3:1-4, 15; 5:5; 6:11; 10:1-13; 11:29-32; Gal 2:17-21; 4:16-21; 5:4, 13; 1 Thess 5:9-10; 2 Thess 3:11-15; Hymenaeus and Alexander (1 Tim 1:19-20); 1 Tim 4:1-3; 5:14-15; 6:20-21; Phygelus and Hermogenes (2 Tim 1:15); Hymenaeus and Philetus (2 Tim 2:17-19); 2 Tim 2:20–21; Heb 5:11-14; 10:38-39; Jas 5:19-20; 1 John 2:28; 5:16-17.

individual in this verse will be "in" the kingdom, that is, saved; but he has not only disobeyed even the least of the commandments, but he has also actively taught others to do the same! He himself not only "disobeys" the Law (Gr *luō*, "to do away with, destroy, bring to an end, abolish,")[58] he actually causes little ones to stumble (as in Matt 18:6). He is a dangerous teacher for he is saying that God said things He did not say, thus incurring the judgment of Jas 3:1. He is a saved person,[59] but will have the lowest status. He finished life as a failure—he is a carnal Christian. As Betz puts it in reference to Matt 5:19:

> One should note that a remarkable paradox results from this evaluation, for, contrary to what one would expect, *a place in the kingdom of God is not denied even to the disloyal teacher who seeks to set aside Jesus' teaching.* Thus, one may assume that in the honorific title 'great'…is promised to a loyal teacher in the heavenly kingdom.[60]

The issue in Matt 5:19 is status, not soteriology.

Pillar 5: Salvation Is by Faith Alone, but Rewards in Heaven Are Obtained by Works.

Shortly after I became a Christian, I was exposed to the idea that the New Testament teaches that God not only saves us by faith alone apart from works, but He also rewards us in heaven based upon our

---

[58] BDAG, s.v. *luō*.

[59] There is a word play on the word *least*. The one who disobeys the least of the commandments will be least in the kingdom. Yet these teachers will be "in" the kingdom. John Nolland is correct when he writes, "being 'least in the kingdom of heaven' still leaves one in the kingdom and not outside it." (John Nolland, *The Gospel of Matthew: A Commentary on the Greek Text* [Grand Rapids: Wm. B. Eerdmans Publishing Co., 2005], p. 222.) Yet Nolland goes on to say in regard to the surpassing righteousness requirement for "entering the kingdom" in v 20, "The threat of exclusion from the kingdom of heaven corresponds closely with the sentiment of verse 19, where, however, the discussion takes place in terms of rank in the kingdom" (*Ibid.*, p. 225.) In other words, he admits that entering the kingdom in verse 20 "corresponds closely" with the idea of rank within the kingdom in verse 19, but then he presents a conflicting view, denying that they correspond closely. Certainly, the ideas of being in the kingdom and therefore saved do not correspond closely with the idea of being excluded from the kingdom altogether.

[60] Hans Dieter Betz and Adela Yarbro Collins, *The Sermon on the Mount: A Commentary on the Sermon on the Mount, Including the Sermon on the Plain (Matthew 5:3-7:27 and Luke 6:20-49)*, Hermeneia (Minneapolis: Fortress Press, 1995), p. 188, emphasis added. Allen agrees: "If any of His disciples taught men to disobey any of its commandments, he would be placed in an inferior position in the coming Kingdom. If he was a faithful servant of the law, and upheld its authority before men, he would receive high rank in the Kingdom." Willoughby C. Allen, *A Critical and Exegetical Commentary on the Gospel According to St. Matthew*, The International Critical Commentary (New York: C. Scribner's Sons, 1907), p. 45.

faithfulness. I remember excitedly going to my pastor to ask him what he thought about this. Instead of sharing my enthusiasm he said, "Jody, God is not a respecter of persons. There is no such thing as rewards in heaven. When the New Testament speaks about rewards, it is always referring to heaven itself, not some crown." He went on to point out, "To seek reward would be a selfish motivation. We are to be motivated only by our love for Christ, not what He can give us."

At the time, I did not know what to say. However, after years of study, I became convinced that the pastor was wrong and that Jesus and the Apostles presented rewards as a key motivator for godly living. It is fair to say the majority of Protestant theologians over the centuries have all held to the doctrine of rewards, although to varying degrees. However, John Piper said in a Sunday morning sermon, "The great error that I am trying to explode in these messages is the error that says, faith in God is one thing and the fight for holiness is another thing. Faith gets you to heaven and holiness gets you rewards."[61]

A prominent evangelical seminary professor complained that the doctrine of differences in eternity future diminishes grace and has a devastating psychological effect on the mental health of sincere Christians. Furthermore, the doctrine in the way the Free Grace interpreters present it, he says, smacks of legalism.

He recounts a conversation with one of his students, in which the student commented that,

> "In most of the conservative Christian circles of which he had been a part, the Christian life was like a free, trial membership to an elite country club: The first year is wonderful, but after that you pay through the nose."[62]

Why is this issue important and how does it relate to the Free Grace Paradigm?

All the Greek words used for reward imply merit of some kind. For example, Jesus says, "For you will be repaid at the resurrection of the righteous" (Luke 14:14). The word for "repay" is *antapodidōmi* and means, "to pay something back to someone as the result of an incurred obligation."[63] God, it seems, has graciously agreed to obligate Himself to pay us wages.

---

[61] John Piper, "Battling the Unbelief of Lust."

[62] Craig L. Blomberg, "Degrees of Reward in the Kingdom of Heaven?," *JETS* 35, no. 2 (1992): 170.

[63] Louw and Nida, *Greek-English Lexicon of the New Testament*, s.v. *antapodidōmi*. See also Col 3:24.

Jesus repeatedly refers to the works of the regenerate man as meriting compensation by using another common term for "wage" (*misthos*) and applying it to the believer's reward in heaven.[64] Seven Greek words are translated "reward," and twenty-nine passages having theological significance related to rewards in the New Testament use *misthos* or cognate Greek words.[65] The basic idea of this word group means payment for work done. For example, "He who receives a prophet in the name of a prophet shall receive a prophet's reward [Gr *misthos*]; and he who receives a righteous man in the name of a righteous man shall receive a righteous man's reward" (Matt 10:41, NASB). The righteous man's "reward" is a *misthos*, "remuneration for work done, *pay, wages*."[66] It is in addition to heaven.

In Rom 4:4, Paul explicitly says that a *wage* is an obligation which is owed to the worker, "Now to the one who works, his wage [Gr *misthos*] is not reckoned as a favor, but as what is due [Gr *opheilēma*]" (Rom 4:4). An *opheilēma* ("what is due") is a "debt" or "obligation."[67] Clearly then, God has agreed to place himself in debt to the faithful Christian when He calls the reward granted a *misthos*. God has obligated Himself to reward work.

Another Greek word for reward is used in Heb 10:35: "Therefore, do not throw away your confidence, which has a great reward [Gr *misthapodosia*]." *Misthapodosia* also refers to "recompense…a payment of wages."[68]

On several occasions Paul refers to a crown the believer may receive at the Judgment Seat of Christ. The victor's crown is obtained only as a result of exceptional performance. He says, "Everyone who competes in the games exercises self-control in all things. They then do it to receive a perishable wreath, but we an imperishable" (1 Cor 9:25, NASB95). The word for "wreath" is *stephanos*, and it refers to an "award or prize for exceptional service or conduct, *prize, reward*."[69]

---

[64] Matt 5:12, 46; 20:28; Luke 6:23; 1 Cor 3:14; 2 John 8.

[65] Harold W. Hoehner, "Rewards," in *New Dictionary of Biblical Theology*, ed. T. D. Alexander and B. S. Rosner (Downers Grove, IL: InterVarsity Press, 2001).

[66] BDAG, s.v. *misthos*, emphasis in original.

[67] Louw-Nida, s.v. *opheilēma*.

[68] BDAG, s.v. *misthapodosia*. See also Heb 11:6, 26.

[69] BDAG, s.v. *stephanos*, emphasis in original. Schreiner and Caneday say, "Each of the crowns is a metaphor for obtaining the heavenly inheritance." (Schreiner and Caneday, *The Race Set Before Us*, p. 83.) Advocates of Free Grace, of course, agree. However, contrary to what these writers believe, the heavenly inheritance is not final entrance into heaven, but, as has been demonstrated in earlier chapters, the inheritance refers to rewards received there.

As discussed above, Paul also says that the inheritance of the believer is a reward (Col 3:24), calling it an *antapodosis*, which means "that which is given to someone in exchange for what has been done, *repaying, reward.*"[70] The writer of the Epistle to the Hebrews tells us that God is a "rewarder" of those who believe Him (Heb 11:6). The Greek word *misthapodotēs* means "one who pays wages."[71]

All these Greek words (*misthos, antapodidōmi, misthapodosia, stephanos, brabeion, antapodosis, misthapodotēs*) express the idea of something obtained by means of effort, remuneration for work done, wages, or payment. They are singularly inappropriate terms to describe a "condition" for final entrance into heaven which comes apart from payment, wages, work done, or remuneration, but instead is obtained "without cost" (Rev 21:6; 22:17). It is therefore lexically implausible to say, as some do, that while believers are judged according to their works, their works have no "merits, but...are the effects of faith."[72] Certainly, they are the effect of abiding in the Vine, but they are also the effect of the believer choosing to abide and to obey (cf. Phil 2:12-13; 4:13).

Because in the Free Grace Paradigm there is a place for works and rewards for faithful service that is different from entrance into heaven by faith alone, one's mind is open to consider these passages in a different manner.

For example, Paul speaks of the reward he hopes to obtain at the Judgment Seat of Christ as a *brabeion*, "Do you not know that those who run in a race all run, but only one receives the prize [Gr *brabeion*]? Run in such a way that you may win" (1 Cor 9:24, NASB95). According to the lexicon, a *brabeion* is "an award for exceptional performance, prize, award."[73] This "prize" is obtained by pressing "on toward the goal for the prize of the upward call of God in Christ Jesus." Some interpreters understand the "prize" as heaven itself and then have a problem that it is obtained by persistent lifelong faith. Free Grace interpreters can take the text at face value and understand the prize as something in addition to heaven based upon works and there is no problem with the faith alone gospel for salvation presented in the New Testament.

---

[70] BDAG, s.v. *antapodosis* emphasis in original.

[71] BDAG, s.v. *misthapodotēs*.

[72] Richard Alderson, *No Holiness, No Heaven!: Antinomianism Today* (Carlisle, PA: Banner of Truth Trust, 1986), p. 100.

[73] BDAG, s.v. *brabeion*. See also Phil 3:14.

Conclusion

My journey from what I believed in graduate school to the acceptance of the Free Grace paradigm took eight years, and it was not easy to arrive at a new destination. However, that destination has been eminently satisfying. Like many others, I came to see many perplexing passages resolved and a coherent, consistent understanding of the New Testament emerged. Furthermore, the distinction between salvation and rewards has profoundly affected how I see life. The Free Grace paradigm urgently challenges us to live life with the end of life in view. How I live now will affect my experience with Christ in eternity future. It will affect my intimacy with him, my opportunities for service, and whether or not I will hear him say, "Well done! Good and faithful servant."[74]

For most of us, paradigm changes are hard. Often there needs to be a precipitating event like there was for me when my Romanian interlocutors challenged me to support my belief in eternal security. For others, it occurs because of persistent nagging doubts about unresolved issues in their paradigm that drive them to finally take a second look. This happened to me as well.

In my own journey, I concluded that there are five key pillars to the Free Grace Paradigm which helped me to satisfactorily explain many passages.

Pillar 1: Salvation is by faith alone and is totally apart from works. Works are condition for discipleship and not all Christians are disciples.

Pillar 2: The Bible teaches that there is a dual-inheritance: One inheritance by faith alone (entrance into heaven, the salvation-inheritance) and one which comes to us by faithfulness of life (the reward-inheritance).

Pillar 3: There are two dimensions to eternal life. It is the gift of regeneration and entrance into heaven by faith alone. But it is also an enhanced experience of life now and in the future as well.

Pillar 4: The existence of the carnal Christian is clearly taught in the Bible. Failure is possible and most of the warnings in the New Testament are directed toward challenging us to avoid that danger.

---

[74] I have discussed the biblical doctrine of rewards in considerable detail elsewhere, Dillow, *Final Destiny*, Chapters 60-65.

Pillar 5: We must distinguish between salvation and rewards. The doctrine of rewards challenges us to live with the end in view. There will be differences in eternity future, greater opportunities for service and intimacy with Christ for those who pursue honor.

This book has attempted to set forth what the authors believe is the best way to understand salvation in the Bible. As we conclude our discussion, there is one question that begs for an answer, "Is the Free Grace paradigm correct?" Obviously the writers of this volume think it is, and we have set forth many reasons for believing it. I, myself, have summarized the results of my own years of reflection on this paradigm in my book *Final Destiny: The Future Reign of the Servant Kings.*

I would like to conclude with my own answer to the question regarding the accuracy of this paradigm. The Free Grace paradigm is true because it has superior explanatory power. What is explanatory power? This "is a quantification of the number of facts the hypothesis can encompass and explain."[75] The efficiency of an interpretive paradigm is simply the number of biblical facts correlated divided by the number of assumptions made. All theories begin with certain initial assumptions, but when many assumptions must be made in order to justify the theory, its explanatory power is useless. In science, "In order to be accepted, any new hypothesis must represent an improvement. It must explain more facts, or provide better explanations of the existing knowledge, than does the older theory."[76] In this regard the Free Grace paradigm succeeds admirably.

When one accepts the five pillars of the Free Grace paradigm, many passages are explained with few assumptions. It is a highly efficient theory. It yields a view of salvation in the Bible that is coherent, consistent, and emerges from the contexts of the passages in question and usage of the words and phrases in those passages found throughout the Bible. Few theological biases are needed. It is highly efficient!

---

[75] John F. Hawley and Katherine A. Holcomb, *Foundations of Modern Cosmology*, 2nd. ed. (Oxford: University Press, 2005), p. 20.

[76] *Ibid.*

APPENDIX - FREE GRACE AND REPENTANCE

Some of the debate about the Free Grace message revolves around the meaning of repentance and whether repentance is necessary for one's justification. Within the Free Grace movement there exist several views regarding repentance; this appendix gives a brief summary of four of the common Free Grace views.[1] A description of the traditional view is included for comparison purposes.

Three of the four Free Grace views (change of mind or heart, internal resolve to turn from one's sins, and regret or admission of guilt) have in common that repentance is an internal change and that it is less than a "turning from sins." They also agree that repentance will normally result in some action, but that action itself is not repentance, i.e., "bearing fruit in keeping with repentance" follows repentance (Matt 3:8, Luke 3:8), in which "in keeping with" means, "pertaining to being fitting or proper in corresponding to what should be expected."[2] The fourth view, (turn from sin) sees cessation of the sinful behavior included in the definition, but does not see repentance as a condition for salvation. All four Free Grace views summarized here are similar in a number of ways (e.g., John the Baptist's call to repent; salvation coming by faith alone in Christ alone, apart from the traditional view of repentance), but they differ in several ways as well.

Traditional Views (Non-Free-Grace)

Wayne Grudem defines repentance as "a heartfelt sorrow for sin, a renouncing of it, and a sincere commitment to forsake it and walk in obedience to Christ."[3] Many outside of the Free Grace camp acknowledge

---

[1] This appendix provides neither a defense or critique of any of those views nor a lexical analysis of the Greek and Hebrew terms involved. The reader is encouraged to consult the cited sources for fuller explanations of each position.

[2] Louw and Nida, *Greek-English Lexicon of the New Testament*, s.v. *axios*.

[3] Grudem, *Systematic Theology*, p. 713.

repentance implies an intellectual component ("changing one's mind so that one's views, values, goals, and ways are changed and one's whole life is lived differently"[4]). Most acknowledge an emotional dimension as well, "a change of feeling manifesting itself in sorrow for sin against a holy and just God."[5] And most include a *necessary* volitional dimension: "genuine repentance *will* effect a change of behavior as well,"[6] or "[S]aving faith will *result* in obedience, and saving faith will include a *sincere resolve to turn from sin* [repentance] *and begin obedience…*"[7] Most who hold the traditional view hold that repentance is a necessary condition for salvation:

> Repentance is a fruit of faith, which is itself a fruit of regeneration. But in actual life, repentance is inseparable from faith, being the negative aspect (faith is the positive aspect) of turning to Christ as Lord and Savior. The idea that there can be saving faith without repentance, and that one can be justified by embracing Christ as Savior while refusing him as Lord, is a destructive delusion.[8]

The Westminster Confession of Faith summarizes the Reformed view of repentance and the necessity of repentance:

> By it [repentance unto life], a sinner…so grieves for, and hates his sins, as to turn from them all unto God, purposing and endeavoring to walk with him in all the ways of his commandments. Although repentance be not to be rested in, as any satisfaction for sin, or any cause of pardon thereof, which is the act of God's free grace in Christ; yet it is of such necessity to all sinners, that none may expect pardon without it.[9]

---

[4] J. I. Packer, *Concise Theology: A Guide to Historic Christian Beliefs* (Wheaton, IL: Tyndale House, 1993). See also L. Berkhof, *Systematic Theology* (Grand Rapids, MI: Wm. B. Eerdmans Publishing Co., 1938), p. 486.

[5] Berkhof, *Systematic Theology*, p. 486.

[6] MacArthur, *The Gospel According to the Apostles*, p. 24, emphasis added.

[7] Wayne Grudem, *"Free Grace" Theology*, p. 71, emphasis his.

[8] J. I. Packer, *Concise Theology*.

[9] *Westminster Confession of Faith*, Chapter 15.1-2. Available online at http://www.opc.org/documents/CFLayout.pdf. Last accessed Sept. 12th, 2016.

Free Grace Views[10]

1. Change of Mind / Change of Heart[11]

> This word remains one of the most troublesome words for
> Bible interpreters who try to remain faithful to the context
> where it is used…[I]t is derived from two Greek words, *meta*
> which means after and *noeō* which means to think. So, we get
> an essential meaning of *after thought* [*sic*] or *change of mind*.[12]

The context must define what a person changes his mind about. It is
not always sin:

> Repentance means a genuine change of mind that affects
> the life in some way. Like other significant theological terms
> it must be defined specifically by asking a further question,
> namely, Change the mind about what? *Unsaved* people can
> truly repent but without being saved, as, for example, to
> change the mind about a bad habit and to break that habit
> as a result. *Christians* can repent of specific sins and stop
> doing them (Rev. 2:5; 2 Cor. 7:9—notice that in this verse
> sorrow leads to repentance, but it is not necessarily the same
> as repentance). And *unsaved* people can repent unto salvation.
> This saving repentance has to involve a change of mind about
> Jesus Christ so that whatever a person thought of Him before,
> he changes his mind and trusts Him to be his Savior. That is
> the only kind or content of repentance that saves (Acts 2:38;
> 17:30; 2 Pet. 3:9).[13]

When John the Baptist and Jesus proclaimed, "Repent, for the kingdom of heaven is at hand," (Matt 3:2; 4:17) the Mosaic Covenant was still
in effect for Israel. This was a call back to covenant for God's covenant

---

[10] Each of the authors cited has agreed that the description of his view is fair and accurate.

[11] See Bing, *Lordship Salvation*, pp. 60-92; *Grace, Salvation, and Discipleship*, pp. 51-52; Charles
Caldwell Ryrie, *Basic Theology: A Popular Systematic Guide to Understanding Biblical Truth*
(Chicago, IL: Moody Press, 1999), pp. 389-90; Richard A. Seymour, "Repentance and the
Free Gift of God" in *Freely By His Grace*, J.B. Hixon, et al, ed. (Duluth, MN: Grace Gospel
Press, 2012); Lewis Sperry Chafer, *Systematic Theology* (Dallas Seminary Press, 1948), 3:372-78;
Robert P. Lightner, Th.D., *Sin, the Savior, and Salvation* (Nashville, TN: Thomas Nelson
Publishers, 1991), p. 167; Robert N. Wilkin, "Repentance as a Condition for Salvation in the
New Testament," Th.D. Dissertation, Dallas Theological Seminary, 1985. He later changed his
view to "turn from sin" (see fn 29).

[12] Bing, *Grace, Salvation, and Discipleship*, p. 51, emphasis added.

[13] Ryrie, *Basic Theology*, pp. 389-90, emphasis added.

people, reminding them that "the way to be restored from departing from God was to repent—to change their minds or attitudes about their sin (Deut. 30:3, 10; 2 Chr. 7:14)."[14]

Bing expands the definition of "change of mind" to avoid thinking of it strictly as an act of the intellect:

> In the New Testament, the word *mind* is used of the inner person, sometimes interchangeably with the word *heart* (cf. Rom. 1:28; 7:23, 25; Eph. 4:17, 23; Col. 2:18). It refers to the seat of decision-making, the unseen part of us that makes us who we are; therefore it is also accurate to translate the word repentance as a *change of heart*.[15]

This explanation helps clarify that the "change of mind" view of repentance implies more than just a change of opinion, but reflects a broader change of perspective.[16]

2. Regret or Admission of Guilt[17]

Dillow writes

> The Gr [sic] word *metanoeō* occurs 14 times in the Septuagint. In each case it is the chosen translation for the Hebrew word *nāham*, to change the mind or feel sorry for. There are 108 uses of *nāham* in the Hebrew Bible and not one of them means 'to turn.' Thus, we should look to *nāham*, 'to regret,' rather than to *shuv*, 'to return,' as the probable background word to the New Testament usage of the *metanoi* word group...This suggests that *metanoeō* refers to regret or admission of guilt, rather than turning from sin.[18]

He addresses repentance in three settings: A call to repentance of the nation of Israel, a call to restoration of fellowship for believers, and a

---

[14] Bing, *Grace, Salvation, and Discipleship*, p. 112.

[15] *Ibid.*, p. 51.

[16] Wayne Grudem, incorrectly, defines this Free Grace view as *"just* a 'change of mind,' (and not any internal resolve to turn from sin)." (Wayne Grudem, *"Free Grace" Theology*, p. 55, emphasis added). The "change of mind" view understands repentance as more than *just* a change of mind and does not limit the object of repentance to sin only.

[17] Dillow, *Final Destiny*, pp. 33-56.

[18] *Ibid.*, pp. 37-38.

preparatory stage leading to saving faith for the unbeliever. Concerning the call to Israel he says, citing 1 Kgs 8:47-50:

> Solomon had in view a national repentance and a national forgiveness of sins. If the nation heeded these calls, they would escape temporal judgment and would be gathered to the land and receive national forgiveness and cleansing... Thus when Jesus said, *"Repent, for the kingdom of heaven is at hand"* (Matthew 3:2), He was calling the nation to repent and receive national forgiveness...If the nation repented (admitted they were wrong) and then brought forth fruits of repentance (changed the behavior), they could avoid the [temporal] "wrath to come."[19]

Concerning the call for believers to repent, he writes:

> Repentance is best understood as an exhortation to Christians to admit their guilt (change their minds about sin), and agree with God (i.e., confess) about them, thus reestablishing fellowship with God through forgiveness (1 John 1:9).[20]

He cites Luke 15:11-32; 2 Cor 7:9-10; 12:21; and Rev 2:5; 3:3, 19 as examples of believers repenting.[21]

Concerning repentance for the unbeliever, he writes:

> A third usage of "repentance" is to admit that one has sinned and to have a sense of regret about it as a necessary precursor to saving faith. This preparatory stage prior to saving faith involves an admission of guilt and one's need for a savior (Matthew 12:41).[22]

> If one defines repentance as an admission of guilt, repentance is clearly necessary for salvation. If one defines repentance as turning from every known sin and submitting to the Lordship of Christ, it is not...Repentance and faith are different things. Repentance can lead to faith, but it does not always do so. Conversely, a refusal to acknowledge one's sin and having no desire to turn from it (regret), blocks the path toward faith and acceptance of God's free offer by faith.[23]

---

[19] *Ibid.*, p. 40.

[20] *Ibid.*, p. 49.

[21] *Ibid.*, p. 48.

[22] *Ibid.*, p. 51.

[23] *Ibid.*, p. 52.

This view acknowledges that the Holy Spirit "convicts the world of sin. That means He brings them to a sense that they are wrong, they are guilty, and they need a Savior. That is repentance."[24]

3. Internal Resolve to Turn from One's Sins[25]

Anderson takes a different approach. He writes:

> Turning from one's sins in an observable manner may well be the *fruit* of repentance and/or believing (compare Acts 3:19 and 11:21), but the turning is not part of the *root*. Yet, if repentance is more than a 'change of mind,' but less than an observable turning from sins, what is it? We suggest this meaning: *an internal resolve to turn from one's sins.* We think this meaning will make good sense in every NT use.[26]

He differentiates between one's relationship with God (justification, which he receives when he believes) and fellowship with God (sanctification, enjoying one's relationship with God). He concludes that repentance is not a condition for receiving eternal life but is instead a condition for fellowship:

> Once again, we ask the question, if repentance is the internal resolve to turn from one's sins, is repentance a condition for receiving eternal life? And once again, we conclude, no. Repentance is not a condition for *receiving* eternal life, but it is a condition for *possessing* eternal life. By possessing eternal life we refer to enjoying a quality of life that only the believer in fellowship with God can have. Repentance is not about relationship; it is about fellowship. In order to "get right with God," one must repent. If an unbeliever is in view, he must believe to receive the free gift of eternal life. He might repent before he believes or after he believes. It is his faith that saves him eternally, but it is his repentance which allows him to enjoy his faith. Repentance concerns fellowship.[27]

Concerning the call of John the Baptist and Jesus to "Repent, for the Kingdom of heaven is at hand," Anderson points out that the nation of

---

[24] *Ibid.*, pp. 55-56.

[25] David R. Anderson, Ph.D., *Free Grace Soteriology*, rev. ed., ed. James S. Reitman (The Woodlands, TX: Grace Theology Press, 2012), pp. 119-59.

[26] *Ibid.*, p. 137, emphasis his.

[27] *Ibid.*, p. 138.

Israel was already in a covenant relationship with God. The appeal of the
prophets for the nation to "return" were appeals to return to covenant loy-
alty to avoid temporal punishment (wrath). He concludes that John the
Baptist, Jesus, and later Peter (in Acts), had dual ministries:

> One was to call the nation of Israel back to fellowship with
> Yahweh. The covenant relationship had long since been estab-
> lished…[they] were all trying to persuade Israel into the repen-
> tance and turning that would restore them to a refreshing fel-
> lowship with God…But the ministry of John, Jesus, and Peter
> was more than calling the nation of Israel to repentance…
> Though the *nation* was called to repentance, *individuals* in the
> nation were called to believe *and* repent.[28]

4. Turn from Sins[29]

Repentance in this view is "a decision to turn from one's sin in order
to escape temporal judgment."[30] Wilkin and Hodges both use examples
such as the Ninevites repenting (Jonah 3:10; cf. Matt 12:41) and unbelievers in the tribulation who do not repent of their murders, etc. (Rev
9:21) to demonstrate that repentance includes the cessation of the negative behavior (sin). The Ninevites "decided to turn from their sins because
they hoped to escape the destruction of their city and the widespread loss
of lives that Jonah had proclaimed."[31] Wilkin concludes that this view fits
every New Testament use of repent.[32]

This view does not see repentance as a condition for salvation:

> The issue in repentance is not who is born again and who is
> not. The issue is who is walking in open rebellion against God
> and who is not. The consequence of turning from one's sins
> is not the gaining of eternal life, but the improvement of and

---

[28] *Ibid.*, p. 158.

[29] Zane C. Hodges, *Harmony with God: A Fresh Look at Repentance* (Dallas: Rendencíon Viva,
2001); *Absolutely Free: A Biblical Reply to Lordship Salvation* (Dallas: Zondervan Publishing
House, 1989), pp. 143-66; Robert N. Wilkin, *The Ten Most Misunderstood Words in the Bible*
(Denton, TX: Grace Evangelical Society, 2012), p. 107-126, "Does Your Mind need Changing?
Repentance Reconsidered," *Journal of the Grace Evangelical Society* 11:20 (Spring, 1998).
Available online at http://faithalone.org/journal/1998i/Wilkin.html. Last accessed Sept. 21,
2016.

[30] Wilkin, *Ten Most Misunderstood Words*, p. 109. See also Hodges, *Harmony*, p. 77.

[31] Wilkin, "Repentance Reconsidered."

[32] Wilkin, *Ten Most Misunderstood Words*, p. 110.

extension of one's life here on earth, whether for the believer or unbeliever.[33]

The proclamation of John the Baptist and, later, Jesus to "repent, for the kingdom of Heaven is at hand" is an issue of national deliverance, not individual regeneration. "Thus, Jesus is calling for national repentance and national faith that the kingdom is at hand…"[34] This national repentance, had it occurred, would not bestow eternal life, but avert temporal judgment by God upon the nation (which did, in fact, happen when Rome attacked the nation in AD 70).

This view distinguishes between "confession of sins" by a believer (1 John 1:9) and repentance by a believer:

> As John's use of repentance in Revelation 2 and 3 makes clear, repentance is for those Christians who have in some way gone astray. The issue is not some failing which is immediately addressed by confession (1 Jn 1:9). The issue is always some prolonged attitude or practice.[35]

> Therefore, as odd as it sounds, repentance should not be a regular part of the life of a believer. Confession is what we should be doing regularly. As long as we are in fellowship with God, the issue for us is confessing our sins as God makes them known to us…[Repentance] is for the believer who is away from God.[36]

Thus, this view understands the call to repentance for both believer and unbeliever alike as a call to turn from sin (cessation of sinful activity) in order to avoid temporal judgment from God, towards a harmonious relationship with God.[37]

---

[33] *Ibid.*, p. 109. See also Hodges, *Harmony*, p. 3.

[34] *Ibid.*, p. 113.

[35] Hodges, *Harmony*, p. 18.

[36] Wilkin, *Ten Most Misunderstood Words*, p. 123.

[37] Hodges, *Absolutely Free*, p. 158.

SCRIPTURE INDEX

About Bold Grace Ministries

Purpose Statement

Bold Grace Ministries exists to: **unite** believers under the banner of God's grace (Eph 4:3-6), **share** the gospel and aid those who will proclaim it faithfully (Rom 10:14-15), **increase** believers' confidence in the power of the indwelling Christ (Gal 2:20), **love** without hypocrisy (Rom 12:9a), **proclaim** the hope of Christ's glorious kingdom (Rom 8:18-21), and **equip** the saints to share Christ's matchless grace and love with others (2 Tim 2:2).

Our Vision

Grace is relevant. By grace God makes Himself available to men, and by grace He meets our deepest needs. Grace unites us, when we are naturally so prone to division. It frees us from pride and the tyranny of sin and effects holiness and humility.

Yet too often grace is missing or downplayed in our message about Christ, our interactions with one another, and our views on the Christian life. By God's grace, and with the help of like-minded brothers and sisters, we hope to reach out to the world with a message of God's free grace, to unite and encourage our brothers and sisters in Christ, and to teach all the ways that His grace is sufficient for us in our pursuit of Christlikeness.

Find more Bold Grace books and learn more about
Bold Grace at www.boldgrace.org.